THE COWBOY SPIRIT

DONNA LIVINGSTONE

GUY WEADICK AND THE CALGARY STAMPEDE

THE COWBOY SPIRIT

GREYSTONE BOOKS

DOUGLAS & McINTYRE

VANCOUVER/TORONTO

Greystone Books
A division of Douglas & McIntyre Ltd.
1615 Venables Street
Vancouver, British Columbia V5L 2H1

Canadian Cataloguing in Publication Data

Livingstone, Donna
   The cowboy spirit

   ISBN 1-55054-488-8

   1. Weadick, Guy. 2. Calgary Stampede—History. 3. Rodeos—Alberta—
Calgary—History. I. Title.
GV1834.56.C'22C3 1996   791.8'4'09712338   C95-911232-4

Editing by Barbara Pulling
Cover and text design by Peter Cocking
Front cover: Illustration by Peter Cocking, based on a photograph of Lloyd Meyers
   on Thunder, Glenbow Archives NA 3181-47. Inset photograph: Guy Weadick,
   Glenbow Archives NA 446-99
Back cover: Guy Weadick, Glenbow Archives NA 446-98
Printed and bound in Canada by Friesens
Printed on acid-free paper

The publisher gratefully acknowledges the assistance of the Canada Council and of
the British Columbia Ministry of Tourism, Small Business and Culture.

This book is dedicated to the memory of Fred Livingstone and Frank Gallup, Buccaneer, Buckaroo.

Contents

The era of the open-range cowboy was brief, but the cowboy became an enduring symbol of opportunity and wide-open spaces.

The Way West

WITH THE CLOSING of the open range in the 1880s, cowboying as a way of life seemed destined for quiet pastures. But the dedication and passion of western writers, artists, performers and promoters brought the cowboy back to the attention of delighted audiences everywhere. And no one was more dedicated or passionate than Guy Weadick. Born at the same time as the American cowboy, Guy devoted his life to keeping cowboy ways alive through vaudeville acts, Wild West shows, silent films and—most spectacularly—the Calgary Stampede. His story *is* the story of the cowboy, and it is through folks like him that the cowboy spirit endures and flourishes.

1

Rochester, New York, is a long way from the rolling foothills of the Rocky Mountains, but on February 23, 1885, it became Guy Weadick's first arena, and he made the most of it.

Smack in the middle of the southern shore of Lake Ontario at the mouth of the Genesee River, a busy shipping port crisscrossed with railway lines and canals, Rochester in the 1880s was a jumping-off point for eager immigrants. It was a city full of energetic young entrepreneurs looking to make their dreams come true.

Rochester people were inventive. The city had weathered several economic depressions through sheer ingenuity. The preponderance of flour mills had given Rochester the nickname of "the Flour City," but when the mills shut down, the residents turned their talents to horticulture and soon had Rochester renamed "the Flower City." Innovations in the clothing and shoe industries, the metalworking and woodworking trades, brewing, the tobacco industry and the manufacturing of patent medicine had allowed Rochester to prosper. Patents abounded: George H. Smith's head lamp, L. S. Graves's elevators, the mail chutes of James Cutler, and Jonathan B. West's water meters. Bausch & Lomb devised a method of framing glass with rubber frames, and not far from the Weadick home, a young George Eastman was developing film and techniques that would change the way people looked at the world.

Guy Weadick's father, George, had been born in the United States of Irish immigrants. He was a switchman on the railway, and it was probably on one of his trips that he met Mary Ann (Minnie), the Irish-Canadian girl who became his wife. The Weadicks lived on the east side of Rochester, the Irish side, where noisy public markets and big new stores rubbed up against the new university. Theirs was a busy, crowded house filled with laughter, lively storytelling and five children. Guy, born in 1885, was the eldest.

Rochester was a talkative town. Four daily newspapers and ten weekly and monthly papers proclaimed the latest news, and topical issues were discussed in heated public debates. Susan B. Anthony led stormy meetings on women's suffrage, and the women's temperance groups commented on public morals. The rich cosmopolitan mix of the population, dominated by Irish and German immigrants, encouraged everyone to speak their minds.

Elaborate travelling circuses were popular, and colourful shows by P. T. Barnum, James A. Bailey, Adam Forepaugh and the Sells Brothers visited Rochester regularly. The large gaily painted wagons pulled into town accompanied by sideshows, music and strange animals, stirring wanderlust among children and adults alike. Rochester was also an important stop on the vaudeville and variety circuit, and acrobats, song and dance skits, comedians and melodrama were a popular part of city life.

However, for young Guy, as for thousands of other young men stretched across the crowded eastern United States, one lone figure dominated the horizon, beckoning with dreams of freedom and independence: the American cowboy.

The cowboy legend had its roots in economics and transportation. After the Civil War and with the completion of the transcontinental railway in 1867, new methods of refrigeration and packing meant that beef could be shipped more economically and efficiently to the eastern United States. However, it was first necessary to bring the cattle to the railheads in Kansas and the northwest. Texas was home to large herds of longhorn cattle, which had been introduced in the eighteenth century by the Spanish. The first cowboys were itinerant workers, often experienced Mexican cowmen or *vaqueros* who passed on their roping and riding skills to ex-slaves and soldiers unemployed after the war.

The era of the open-range cowboy lasted about thirty years, from the 1860s to the 1890s. During this period, cattle were allowed to roam freely until they were gathered during spring roundups, branded, sorted and trailed north to the railway towns. Many of the large Texas ranches, such as the Matador or the XIT, were owned by corporations with local managers. Experienced cowboys who could work cattle well became "top hands" and enjoyed a sense of personal freedom knowing they could be hired anywhere.

However, a series of severe winters, bad droughts and overstocked ranges in the 1880s caused ranchers to reconsider their operations. Barbed-wire fencing sprang up to keep cattle closer during cold weather. Cowboys found themselves working fields of hay and alfalfa to provide winter feed for cattle, and homesteaders began staking claims and building their own fencing. A direct rail link was established between central Texas and the meat markets of Chicago, and by the 1890s the days of the open range and the long cattle drives were over. The work of the cowboy continued, however, in Texas and throughout the northwest and into Canada. The skills learned on the range were honed and adapted for local conditions, and these would endure.

The cowboy also took on another, unexpected role in the 1880s. Through the new accessibility of printing presses and lithography, with the popularity of Wild West melodramas on stage and screen and in the hands of nostalgic artists such as Charlie Russell and Frederic Remington, this illiterate, taciturn labourer on horseback became a national hero.

Easterners such as the Weadicks first received word of the cowboy from friends and relatives who had made their way west to Wyoming, Texas, Montana and California. In sporadic letters home and on occasional visits, they spoke of a life where a man could live or die by his own wits, and where scattered stars and lowing cows provided the only companionship. To a population crammed into noisy and odorous cities, this was a breath of freedom, a glimpse of the possibilities for which they had come to America.

First-hand reports were backed up by a growing number of published accounts written by those who had lived the cowboy life. One of the first was by Charles Suringo, who described himself as "an old stove up cowpuncher who has spent nearly twenty years on the great western cattle ranges." Born in Texas in 1855, Suringo drove herds to Kansas and worked as a cowboy in New Mexico. His book, *A Texas Cowboy or 15 Years on the Hurricane Deck of a Spanish Pony*, published in 1885, delighted readers with the "straight goods" on life on the open range. In turn, Suringo was delighted with the new interest in cowboys. His purpose in writing the book, he stated flatly, was "money—and lots of it." His stories may have been somewhat exaggerated, but the language was new, iconoclastic and invigorating.

Theodore Roosevelt's 1888 autobiography, *Ranch Life and the Hunting-Trail*, established the cowboy style. The illustrations by Frederic Remington brought the cowboy to life. The artist's quick, laconic lines showed readers how the cowboy dressed, the landscape in which he rode and the scenes of his daily life, and Roosevelt's crisp language served as a call to arms for young

The Log of a Cowboy

Exasperated by the cowboy antics he had seen portrayed in a western play, Texas cowboy Andy Adams decided to describe his experiences on the long cattle drive up to Kansas. His classic account *The Log of a Cowboy* (1903) gives a glimpse into authentic life on a cattle drive: "We had a splendid camp-fire that night, of dry live oak logs, and after supper was over and the first guard had taken the herd, smoking and story telling were the order of the evening. The camp-fire is to all outdoor life what the evening fireside is to domestic life. After the labors of the day are over the men gather around the fire, and the social hour of the day is spent in yarning. The stories told may run from the sublime to the ridiculous, from a true incident to a base fabrication, or from a touching bit of pathos to the most vulgar vulgarity."

Published accounts of authentic life on the western range by such authors as Theodore Roosevelt fired the public imagination and contributed to the growing popularity of the cowboy.

men. The cowboy life, said the man Americans would later call "the Cowboy President," "is superbly health-giving, and is full of excitement and adventure, calling for the exhibition of pluck, self-reliance, hardihood, and dashing horsemanship; and of all forms of physical labor the easiest and pleasantest is to sit in the saddle."

By the 1890s, the cowboy was everywhere. He was popularized in illustrated papers such as the *Police Gazette* and *Frank Leslie's Illustrated Weekly*. He was a promoter's gold mine. Stories by writers such as Peter B. Kyne, Prentiss Ingraham, Samuel S. Hall and Gerald Carlton sold by the thousands.

The cowboy also appeared in popular verse. Poets found rich material in the powerful sentimentality of the "passing West," and their poetry often reflected the ballad tradition of cowboy songs. Cowboys riding herd on the range or during the long cattle drives sang to cattle to soothe them. The subjects of such songs as "Little Joe the Wrangler," "The Cowboy's Lament" and "The Chisholm Trail" reappeared in published cowboy verse with the language cleaned up for public taste. Wallace Coburn's 1903 book of poems, *Rhymes from a Round-Up Camp*, had a plaintive yet bracing message:

Out on the prairie's rolling plain,
No matter what the weather,
My horse and I will live or die,
For work we must together.

Though far from the doctor's skilful art,
We quaff the wine of freedom,
And feel the wealth of perfect health,
By trust in Nature's wisdom.

The cowboy's dry sense of humour also emerged. B. M. Bower's book, *Chip of the Flying U*, published in 1904 and illustrated by Charles M. Russell, took a more lighthearted fictional view of life on the range, but the sentiments were pure cowboy. In it, Chip expresses his disdain for eastern dudes.

> "I wish I had the making of the laws. I'd put a bounty on all the darn fools that think they can write cowboy stories just because they rode past a round-up once, on a fast train," he growled, reaching for a tobacco sack. "Huh! I'd like to meet up with the yahoo that wrote that rank yarn! I'd ask him where he got his lack of information. Huh! A cow-puncher togged up like he was going after the snakiest bronk in the country, when he was only going to town in a buckboard! 'His pistol belt and drink and leathern chaps'—oh, Lord; oh Lord! And spurs! I wonder if he thinks it takes spurs to ride a buckboard? Do they think, back East, that spurs grow on a man's heels out here and won't come off? Do they think we sleep in 'em, I wonder?"

Cowboy farces and melodramas dominated Broadway theatres from the 1890s to 1908, and cowboys began to appear in the flickering new film medium. Bronco Billy Anderson became the first western film star in 1903 with *The Great Train Robbery*, while in the same year, Owen Wister's classic *The Virginian* appeared on Broadway.

But the greatest of the western figures who shaped the growing cult of the cowboy was William F. "Buffalo Bill" Cody. In this legendary entrepreneur and entertainer, the reality and myth of the West blended dramatically to satisfy the dreams and expectations of every audience. Cody was authentic: a

Cowboy Movies

Early western films adopted the formula plots of popular dime novels, Wild West shows and stage melodramas. They were two-reelers, about half an hour in length, with the screen action underscored by piano music and dramatic captions. Early film stars such as "Bronco Billy" Anderson and William S. Hart represented the two forms the cowboy would take: the boyish, hard-shooting daredevil cowboy and the strong silent type, modelled after the Virginian. Wild West performers such as Tom Mix, Buck Jones, Ken Maynard and Yakima Canutt, among others, also took to the screen, where their riding and sharpshooting skills made them instant stars. Movie horses like Tarzan, shown here with Ken Maynard, became stars in their own right.

scout, a mountain man and an Indian fighter whose adventures had been documented in countless books and articles. In Buffalo Bill, the drawings of Remington and Russell came to breathtaking life. His flowing moustache, long hair and goatee were topped with a wide-brimmed ten-gallon Stetson hat—a hat that he introduced and made into an icon. He rode into arenas with casual grace, wearing skin-tight white trousers, thigh-high black leather boots, a wide leather belt with an oversized silver buckle, an embroidered shirt, a fringed and beaded leather jacket and enormous leather gauntlets.

"I'm coming," promised a French poster, and European audiences waited eagerly for Buffalo Bill's thrilling Wild West.

His appearance was as exotic as a circus act, yet born on American soil out of American ingenuity. He was irresistible.

In 1872 Cody entered show business when he accepted an invitation to appear in a frontier melodrama produced by Ned Buntline. Entitled "The Scouts of the Prairies or Red Deviltry As It Is," the program featured a young Virginian named John Burwell Omohundro Jr., who played Texas Jack and shared the stage with Buffalo Bill. The play was a rootin', tootin' spectacle of shooting tricks, western skits, Indian dances, a knife fight, a dramatic rescue, a prairie fire and roping demonstrations.

The show travelled from Chicago to New York and appeared in Rochester, where Buffalo Bill and Omohundro extended their stage presence into the local bars. Dressed in fringed western buckskins, they would thrill listeners with hair-raising stories of the West and occasionally gallop down the city's main street, shooting and yelling to the amusement and fright of passersby.

Buffalo Bill teamed up with promoter Nate Salsbury, who saw an even wider arena for Cody. Salsbury proposed a show that would tell the whole panoramic outdoor story of the West as it was—the thrilling events, the cowboys, the Indians, the superb horsemanship—a real account, too, not some circus affair or showbiz farce.

Cody tested the idea in his hometown of North Platte, Nebraska, on July 4, 1882. He organized what he called "The Old Glory Blow Out," in which more than a thousand cowboys competed in exhibitions of riding, roping and shooting. The show was the forerunner of the rodeo, and it delighted audiences and competitors alike.

It was also the forerunner of Cody's famous "Buffalo Bill Wild West," a spectacular combination of western tableaux, sharpshooting, trick riding and roping, Indian pageants, historical reenactments and gunfights that went on to thrill Queen Victoria and audiences around the world. Cody dominated the emerging Wild West business from the 1880s to his final appearance in 1916, and his name alone was enough to guarantee a crowd.

The West was changing, and in 1893 the Chicago World's Columbian Exposition was unsuspecting host to the transition that was taking place. Just outside the fair, Buffalo Bill expanded his Wild West to include an

"International Congress of Roughriders of the World." But even as these performers presented the nostalgia of the Old West, within the fair gates American historian Frederick Jackson Turner was presenting his classic paper "The Significance of the Frontier in American History" to a startled group of American historians. The American frontier was gone, Turner declared, and with it the opportunity of beginning again. Instead, the spirit of the frontier had been absorbed into the American consciousness. But if the frontier was gone, the responsibility for preserving its memory was being passed on to a new generation. In Buffalo Bill's audience, a teen-aged Will Rogers, soon to be known as the Cherokee Kid, watched enthralled as Mexican roper Vincente Orapeza worked his magic.

In the wake of Buffalo Bill's model, Wild West shows sprang up across the country in the first years of the new century. They fed a public appetite for "authentic" depictions and usually drew their performers from working cowboys, ranchers and well-known Indian figures. More than a hundred shows ranging from small local operations to large-scale productions with more than a touch of circus to them travelled the country and Europe. Among the best-known of these were Pawnee Bill's Wild West, Cummins's Wild West and Indian Congress and, from Bliss, Oklahoma, the Miller Brothers 101 Ranch Real Wild West.

For Guy Weadick, growing up in the bustle of Rochester, even better than the exploits of Buffalo Bill, more thrilling than Wild West shows and more exciting than the dime novels of Bronco Billy were the stories told by his uncles visiting from California and Wyoming. From them, he heard stories of cattle, Indians, horses and cowboys, and of a western landscape that stretched as far as the eye could see. He became determined to see it all for himself.

Cowboy Artists

Missouri-born Charles M. Russell (shown left) headed to Montana when he was sixteen. For the next ten years, he worked as a cowboy and began capturing the events of cowboy life in sketches, paintings or wax models. The vividness and accuracy of his work soon attracted national attention, and his images appeared in popular books and magazines. Like his fellow artist Frederic Remington, he wanted to capture forever the traditional cowboy life he saw disappearing around him.

Yale-educated Remington first went west in 1881. His sketches from that trip were published in *Harper's Weekly*, and he soon became an accomplished western artist. He was concerned about the passing of the Old West and wanted to represent the life of the cowboys he admired. Remington's cowboys were drawn in detail and alive with action, and he frequently depicted native Indian life and cavalry scenes.

Far from the vaudeville antics of Bronco Billy and the Wild West of Buffalo Bill, cowboys on the western range continued to rope cattle, ride herds, break wild horses and work roundups in the traditional way.

The Birth of a Promoter

2

GUY WAS A TEEN-AGER WHEN he headed west, a gangly, gregarious kid with a hank of hair always in his eyes and an open grin. As he travelled from the Dakotas and Montana to the Mexican border, he picked up work along the way.

The West that Guy entered was in transition. The days of the open range were gone, but there were still plenty of cowboys around who could tell stories of the days before the arrival of barbed wire. Guy learned about horses. He learned about resourcefulness and standing on your own two feet and settling your own problems. He learned about cowboy humour, often at his own expense. Always he liked best to listen to the old-timers, men who could read the land and the sky and a cow's eye as clearly as a book. What he learned stayed with him all his life.

As he worked and watched and listened, Guy picked up range skills—breaking wild horses, roping horses, cows and calves, wrestling three-year-old steers to the ground. He noticed, too, that many of these skills were moving from the land to the stage. Trick ropers, bronc busters and steer wrestlers who had competed informally in ranch roundups were now packing their gear and their livestock and appearing on the vaudeville circuits and on stages as far away as London and New York.

At the turn of the century, the United States was entering the "Progressive Era," in which the country's urban population grew four times as fast as that of the rural areas. Theodore Roosevelt, elected as U.S. president in 1901, was casting an expansionist eye abroad. Amid the clamour over social reform, education, public health issues, social Darwinism, electricity and the Panama Canal, the cowboy voice was becoming lost or ignored. The American West, the last frontier, as Frederick Jackson Turner had predicted, was disappearing from most people's minds.

However, those who lived in the western landscape fought to preserve its traditions and customs. Artists such as Charles Russell and Frederic Remington cast their clear eyes around them and painted as fast as they could. Writers like Zane Grey and Max Brand kept the western story alive in their books. The burgeoning Wild West shows and western vaudeville acts and movies attempted to capture a way of life that seemed to be slipping through their fingers.

But there was still much for Guy Weadick to see. The West has its own ceremonies, its own pageantry, and in 1904 Guy witnessed a spectacular event.

The Blood people near Standoff, Alberta, south of Macleod, were hosting their annual Sun Dance Ceremony, and thousands of visitors from the nearby Gleichen Reserve, Peigans from Brocket in southern Alberta and Montana Blackfeet were gathering. Colourful costumes, haunting music, decorated tipis and thousands of horses filled the landscape. Guy, in the area on a horse-buying trip with some Montana cowboys, was struck by the grandeur of the event.

While attending the ceremony, Guy met Crop-Eared Wolf, head chief of the Bloods. There was a fad at the time for having your photograph reproduced on a button, and Guy had a button of himself to which the chief took a fancy.

In 1908, immigration brochures promised a land of natural abundance, bountiful crops and homesteads for the future at reasonable prices.

14

Guy made Crop-Eared Wolf a present of the button, and the chief wore it constantly from then on. He often told people that it was a photo of his son.

Guy was now twenty years old, well travelled, and he was getting to know many of the cowboys and ranches in the southern Alberta and Montana area. This was "big sky" country, where rolling foothills were protected by the eastern slopes of the Rocky Mountains and chinook winds warmed the winters. Although the development of ranching was different in Canada, cowboy work was pretty much the same on either side of the border.

Ranching in western Canada began in the 1880s with the arrival of the railway. Generous land leases and a growing demand for beef attracted investors from eastern Canada and Britain. Soon the foothills and western grasslands were dotted with cattle and horses carrying the brands of such well-known ranches as the Cochrane, the North-West Cattle Company, the Oxley, the Waldrond, the Quorn, the Winder, the OH and the Military Colonization Ranch. Among the first ranchers were the "Queen's Cowboys," former members of the North-West Mounted Police who had come west in 1884 to bring order to the whisky traders and establish peaceful relations with the native peoples of the plains.

Roping and riding competitions were a popular form of entertainment in cattle country, whether they were the formal events staged annually around Cheyenne Frontier Days, Prescott Frontier Days and the Pendleton Roundup, or small local events in which riders rode into the arena fresh from their range work.

The earliest noted cowboy event of this kind in Calgary took place in June 1893, when well-known rancher and cowman George Lane of the Bar U Ranch organized a series of "interesting cowboy sports" during the annual summer agricultural fair. *The Calgary Weekly Herald* noted that

> The exhibition was entirely new to probably a majority of those present and they watched the sport with the keenest enjoyment. The horses bestrode by the cowboys were important factors in the contest. The hardy little brutes seemed to be possessed of human intelligence and the manner in which they performed their allotted parts was a revelation.

The Bar U Ranch

In 1882, Montreal investors, spurred on by the urgings of Fred Stimson, an experienced stockman, founded the North-West Cattle Company, one of the most important cattle organizations in western Canada. Known far and wide as the Bar U Ranch, the operation was originally stocked by 3,000 head of cattle and 75 horses driven in from Idaho. The ranch was later bought by Gordon, Ironsides & Fares and ably managed by George Lane. Under Lane's direction, the ranch prospered and became known for its Percheron horses and other stock. In 1920, Lane bought out his partners. He operated the ranch successfully until his death in 1925.

The roping of range cattle by the cowboys—genuine cowboys straight from the roundup—is a new feature in the exhibition and one that cannot fail to attract visitors from all parts; it is one, too, that is characteristic of the Northwest especially, and will be particularly interesting not to strangers merely but to our own people as well, since so few residents of town really know anything of range life.

The cowboy competition at the Calgary fair proved so popular it was brought back the following year. Bronc riding joined the roping events, and audiences were treated to some breathless competition.

The cattle country of southern Alberta was rich in top riders and ropers. The Austin boys—Frank, Gus, Jim, Dave, Lee and Paul of Cardston—were known on both sides of the border. Jim, who performed as "the Montana Kid," was acknowledged as the top rider of the bunch. One of his stunts, as described by Guy Weadick, was to place "a silver dollar under each foot in the stirrups and hold the coins there until he had completed ridin,' whippin' and scratchin' a notorious hell-raiser, every jump—until it quit pitching, broke and ran." The steer-throwing abilities of John Ware, a former slave who had come north from Texas in a cattle drive in the 1880s and stayed to work on Alberta ranches, were legendary.

In the fall of 1904, Guy saw some impressive performances at a riding and roping competition in Cardston. Ray Knight of Raymond, Alberta, who won the steer roping prize, had already made a name for himself in the rodeo business. In 1902, he and rancher Addison "Ad" Day had organized the Knight and Day rodeo in Raymond, said to be the first of its kind in the country. The Austin boys were on hand in Cardston for the bronc riding, as well as "Pretty Boy" Anderson of Lethbridge. Guy made friendships and contacts here that would last throughout his life.

These local competitions weren't formal affairs. The rules were general, and most of the competitors were working cowboys who had learned their performing "tricks" as a matter of survival. Riding a mean bronc in a ranch yard didn't mean lowering yourself into a chute where the horse was hobbled down and already saddled as it would in later rodeo competitions.

George Lane was one of southern Alberta's most respected ranchers and one of the Big Four who supported Guy's vision for the Stampede.

And the working cowboy's ride didn't end with an eight-second whistle. Instead, as rancher Bert Sheppard later described it in an article in *Canadian Cattlemen*, "they had to take a beetle-headed bronc, saddle it, go out on the range and do a day's work on it and eventually teach the horse something worth while."

These events, carried out for the most part in working ranch arenas or on open grasslands, were watched critically, and it was only the top rider who won respect from such knowledgeable onlookers.

Skilled riders brought their talents from the ranch into the rodeo arena. The popular Joe LaMar could clear a fallen horse by turning a backward somersault over the saddle, landing on his feet. Rod Redfern could throw his leg halfway over the saddle, keep hold of the horn and ride his bronc to a standstill with his body down alongside the horse.

In 1905, Guy was back in Alberta to attend the Calgary Exhibition with some Montana cowboys and the Austin brothers. For Guy, the big attraction was the opportunity to meet and talk with real rangemen. Alberta was in the midst of a population boom, brought on by Immigration Minister Clifford Sifton's new immigration policy. The majority of immigrants were farmers from Ontario, the United States and Britain. Calgary was a service and market centre for the farming and ranching community, but it was already looking ahead to developing as a progressive commercial and industrial city.

From Calgary, Guy drifted south to Cheyenne for its annual Frontier Days, then on to Fort Worth, Texas, where he attended the Fat Stock Show. It was here that Guy teamed up with one of the most unusual acts in western show history, an act that would quickly become the breathless focus of rodeos throughout the U.S.

Bill Pickett was a black brush-country cowboy, possibly part Cherokee, born about 1863 in Williamson County, Texas. One day in 1903 to save his horse from being gored, Bill leaped from his horse and wrestled a steer to the ground, biting the steer's upper lip. It worked so well he tried it again, and he soon began appearing in various events around the country to demonstrate his new-found skill. He became known as the Dusky Demon, and his dangerous but effective feat captured audiences wherever he performed.

The Daddy of 'Em All!

Cheyenne, Wyoming, began as a cattle town servicing the great Texas herds and developing a flourishing beef industry on the rail line. In 1897, local ranchers and businesspeople decided to celebrate their colourful western heritage by staging a huge cowboy contest. The *Cheyenne Sun Leader* predicted that the proposed Frontier Days would be a "marker from which to reckon all events." It was, and it has since gone on to became an annual event, known as "the Daddy of 'Em All." A full program of rodeo events attracts top contestants from all over North America, and military performances, top musical acts, automobile races and special appearances by screen stars have rounded out the schedule, attracting thousands of visitors every summer.

Bill Pickett's unique biting bulldogging act thrilled audiences across North and South America and Europe.

Guy announced and promoted Pickett's unique act at the Fort Worth Fat Stock Show, billing it as bulldog bite-'em style. In the audience was a man who was to shape the careers of both Weadick and Pickett. Zack Miller was in town looking for stock for the 101 Ranch in Oklahoma. The 101 Ranch was an impressive, self-sufficient empire run as a family partnership by Zack and his two brothers, Joseph and George, after the death of their father, George, in 1903.

The Millers were risk-takers who adhered to a basic business philosophy: "It is just as bad to go broke in a little way as it is in a big way." Their 110,000-acre ranch sprawled across four counties in north-central Oklahoma and encompassed cattle ranching, oilfields, grassland, schools, churches, roads, and a telephone and mail system that linked the 101 headquarters to foremen on the distant range. At the 101 Ranch store, "everything from a needle to a Ford car" could be bought and paid for by hired hands with 101 folding money and coins.

Zack Miller was also in Fort Worth to rustle up acts for an event that would establish the reputation of the 101 Ranch on a national scale. In June 1905, the ranch would host the annual convention of the National Editorial Association, a group of leading newspaper editors, reporters and publishers. When Weadick and Pickett signed on with Miller, they became performers in one of the most spectacular private displays of western stunts ever presented.

The Miller brothers were master promoters. They papered the country with announcements and invited every writer and celebrity they could think of to attend the shindig. There was considerable talent already on the ranch, and many a 101 hand later appeared on the Wild West, vaudeville and movie circuits. When the convention opened at the ranch on June 11, more than 64,000 spectators were on hand to witness—and to write about—the Miller Brothers Wild West Show.

The heroes of the West were paraded around the ring. An elderly Geronimo, who was serving as a prisoner of war at Fort Sill, was brought in to kill a buffalo for a barbecue. Lucille Mulhall, described by Will Rogers as "the first cowgirl," galloped around the grandstand performing the stunts that had won her the title of world's lady roping champion at Cheyenne and

Pendleton. Parades, rodeo events, and Indian raids on stagecoaches and wagon trains filled out the program.

Guy Weadick's announcement was the most thrilling of the day: "Ladies and gentlemen. The next event will be Bill Pickett, the Dusky Demon from Texas, who will leap from the back of a running horse onto a running steer and throw the steer with his bare hands and teeth."

A thousand-pound steer ran onto the field at full speed, followed closely by a mounted hazer whose job it was to keep the steer running straight and in front of the grandstand. Then, in spectacular fashion, Bill Pickett galloped into the ring, dressed as a Spanish bullfighter. Pickett was in his prime, a slim, toughened cowboy with powerful shoulders and arms. In minutes he had ridden up and caught the huge wild steer, twisting him over and biting his lip to subdue him. The crowd roared its approval as Guy and Bill grinned at each other.

The next day, George Miller arranged for some movie shots of the ranch. They needed a daredevil cowboy to ride a horse off a bluff and through a flood-swollen stream. Tom Mix, who was working on the ranch, began his movie career with this foolhardy stunt. He blindfolded his horse, rode forty or fifty yards away from the bluff, wheeled, rode off the bluff into the river and swam the horse over to the north bank. Guy got to know Tom at the ranch and formed a lasting friendship with the cowboy performer.

Every major newspaper and magazine in the country covered the colourful blow-out at the 101 Ranch. The public response was immediate and enthusiastic, and during the next few years, the Miller brothers put together the 101 Ranch Real Wild West, one of the most impressive travelling shows of its kind, rivalling the legendary Buffalo Bill in attracting audiences.

Weadick and Pickett were anxious to take their act on the road. They headed north to Alberta, where they were hired by western promoters Creswell & Osborne to put together some shows in the Calgary area. Guy was a natural at publicity, and the shows went over well. Although Pickett was paid a flat sum each week to perform, he was so pleased at the way his stunt was received in Airdrie, just outside of Calgary, that he bulldogged two extra steers, as he said, "just to be sociable."

A Star Cowboy

Tom Mix was tall, dark and handsome, and he never turned away from trouble. Mix had been a sheriff, a deputy U.S. marshall, a ranch foreman, a soldier and a Wild West performer with the Miller Brothers 101 Ranch. With his famous horse, Tony, he blazed a path of cowboy justice in more than 300 films from 1909 to 1934. He performed his own stunts and would ride Tony over crumbling bridges or leap onto runaway stagecoaches with casual grace.

At the height of his career in the 1920s, Mix's salary was $7,500 a week. He loved diamonds and fast cars, and he owned a $40,000 mansion with his initials flashing in neon at the entrance. In 1929, he and actor William S. Hart were pallbearers at Wyatt Earp's funeral.

The Miller Brothers 101 Ranch Real Wild West, launched in 1905, attracted huge audiences wherever it appeared.

In July 1905, Bill Pickett was presented by Guy Weadick to audiences at the Calgary Exhibition. Once again, Bill dressed in the gold-trimmed toreador pants and black silk stockings of a Spanish bullfighter. He was an exciting sight, but the act he performed outshone his costume. Guy used a megaphone and all the hyperbole of a circus ringmaster to whip up excitement during the performance, describing each action in thrilling terms and warning onlookers what to expect. But not everyone was thrilled with the performance. Protests from the pulpit were echoed in an editorial in Calgary's *Daily Herald*, which declared that "when a man is permitted to make an exhibition of this character in the presence of women and children, the finer sensibilities are outraged."

Creswell & Osborne were pleased with the response, however, and decided to put together a western act that could appear in towns across the Canadian prairies. They added some longhorn steers and good bucking horses to Weadick and Pickett's act and shipped the outfit off to Winnipeg, where they hoped to first contract the show for the Winnipeg Exhibition. The Exhibition people had already booked their grandstand attractions. But with a bit of smooth talking, Guy arranged with the management of River Park, on the other side of town from the exhibition grounds, to allow the western show to perform. Despite the considerable drawing power of the exhibition, the little show did a thriving business each evening.

During the show's Winnipeg run, Guy made the rounds, meeting everyone he could, including J. T. Gordon and W. H. Fares of the firm Gordon, Ironside & Fares, the Winnipeg packers and ranchers who shared an interest in the famous Bar U Ranch in southern Alberta.

Unfortunately, disaster soon overtook the little Wild West show. Arriving at the grounds one afternoon, Weadick and Pickett discovered that their horses and cattle were missing, along with their chaps, saddles, bridles, blankets and spurs. By asking around, they discovered that their steers had been sold early that morning at the Winnipeg Stockyards. Two men had been seen trailing a bunch of horses south.

In the dramatic style of a Ned Buntline melodrama, Weadick and Pickett caught the night train to Emerson, Manitoba, crossed over into Pembina, North Dakota, and began making inquiries. The sheriff reported passing two men answering the description on the road heading east into Pembina earlier that day. When the riders and horses appeared, they were positively identified by Guy and Bill. The two men were taken to the local jail by the sheriff, and the horses and equipment placed in custody until the matter was investigated.

The capture had mixed results for Weadick and Pickett. Since their saddles and gear had been brought across the line illegally, they were subject to seizure and sale by advertised auction. The boys would have to wait for a chance to bid on their own property. They shrugged, grumbled a bit at the cussedness of the law and headed south.

Pickett continued on to Texas, where he ended up with a party of top American cowboys headed to Argentina to compete against Argentinean gauchos. From all reports, Pickett's exhibition of bulldogging a steer once again thrilled spectators.

As for Guy, he stopped at Chicago, where he took in another Wild West show—and roped in a partner for life.

Weadick & LaDue, rope twirlers par excellence.

Weadick & LaDue

THE Col. Fred. T. Cummins Wild West and Indian Congress was playing an engagement at White City, the former site of the World's Fair, when Guy Weadick arrived in Chicago in the fall of 1905.

Fred Cummins had grown up among native peoples and had been a trader, prospector, cowboy and bronc breaker in such places as Deadwood, Helena, the Coeur-d'Alene country and Standing Rock Agency. Using his contacts with the federal Indian Bureau, he had initially developed a touring ethnographic exhibition featuring different tribes of native peoples, including, at various times, Geronimo and other Apache prisoners of war; Red Cloud, Oglala Sioux chief in the war of 1868; and Chief Joseph of the Nez Perce. For many aboriginal peoples, the Wild West shows offered an economic option

3

that was more appealing than being confined to the restrictions of reservation life or prison. By the time Guy met up with the show in 1905, Cummins had expanded his program to incorporate Wild West elements and, like many other shows of the time, some circus elements. Guy was very taken with the show—and particularly with a spirited young trick rider, Miss Flores LaDue.

The following spring Guy returned to Winnipeg, where he was contracted to stage a Wild West show in a big summer amusement park called Happyland. After the season there concluded, he hurried south, to catch up with the Cummins show and woo the trick rider who had caught his fancy.

Guy Weadick and Flores LaDue met in Iowa in October. Five weeks later, on November 17, 1906, they were married at Memphis, Tennessee, where Flores was staying with a cousin. Flores was twenty-three and Guy was twenty-one.

Flores LaDue, or Florence as she was known, was born Grace Maud Bensell in Montevideo, Minnesota, on June 17, 1883, the only child of Charles Bensell, a wealthy criminal lawyer who later became a judge. Charles Bensell had been raised on the Sioux reservation at Fairbault, Minnesota, where his father had been the first government Indian agent. Bensell owned a number of farms and ranches in Minnesota and South Dakota, so Grace was around horses from an early age. She became an expert rider. In later years, she called herself "the boy of the family."

Her mother had died when she was young, and Grace Maud seemed born with a gypsy heart. A few years before meeting Guy Weadick, she had run away from home, apparently to join the circus. One day, after her father had gone out, she called a carriage to take her baggage and followed along behind it, sweeping away her tracks in the snow so she couldn't be followed.

Colonel Cummins was a personal friend of Charles Bensell's, and Grace Maud first took to the stage in Cummins's show. Under the name of Flores or Florence LaDue, she was very popular with audiences. Her flashing eyes and skill with a horse caught the eye of Will Rogers, who invited her to perform her fancy roping tricks with the one-man combination show he was attempting to put together for the vaudeville circuit. She performed with his short-lived act until Rogers learned that his real talent was as a solo performer, giving audiences his personal view of the nation's affairs.

Cowgirls

Women performed and competed regularly with men in both rodeo events and Wild West shows. Many cowgirls preferred to ride "slick" without tying the stirrups beneath the horse to hobble it. Riding slick was more dangerous, but a cowgirl could earn extra points that way. In Wild West performances, most cowgirls designed showy outfits to dazzle the crowd. But in competitions, costumes had to be comfortable and sleek, with no fringes or decorations that could catch on running hoofs or dangling stirrups. Yet they had to be modest to avoid shocking crowds already startled to see female competitors. Florence LaDue, Lucille Mulhall and many other cowgirls wore practical, divided ankle-length skirts during competitions. Others, like Tillie Baldwin and Hazel Walker, shocked crowds with their harem pants and pantaloons, which allowed them to do headstands and other trick riding with greater ease and safety.

Flores LaDue twirled her way from vaude-ville stage to Wild West arenas, world champion lady fancer roper and dude rancher with western style and flair.

Guy and Florence made an attractive couple. He was tall and slim, and she was tiny, not more than five feet, and athletic as a cat. He was the consummate promoter, talking to everyone, soaking up every publicity angle, swapping stories. Her large eyes were warm and friendly, and she knew her own mind. They decided to team up on stage.

Florence was accomplished as both a trick and a fancy roper. Guy by now was a trick roper himself. He probably learned his roping tricks on the range, and he honed them during his years on the vaudeville circuit, where western acts were popular.

Weadick and LaDue's act was about fifteen minutes in length and full of action. Guy and Florence would send large rope loops spinning in the air, then jump through the coils or twist the long ropes into knots. Guy's rope would sail out to encircle Florence, and in minutes she would be tied from head to foot. They had horses in their act, and Florence would rope the animals or spin a fancy lariat from horseback. All the while Guy would deliver a teasing patter.

A Dynamic Duo

Guy and Florence were in their early twenties when they took their act on the vaudeville circuit. Emulating the style of Will Rogers, they combined trick and fancy roping with a humorous patter. Show people with cowboy spirit, they made many contacts that would later serve them well as they organized stampedes and operated their dude ranch.

Wherever they went, they took the time to pick up new skills and to make improvements on their roping tricks. They had the opportunity to learn from the best: Tex McLeod, Chester Byers, Sam Garrett and Hank Durnell were regarded as the "Big Four" of roping, and along with Joe Barrera and other famed ropers, worked their tricks for the Miller Brothers and other western shows. At the time, roping and riding alternated regularly between vaudeville and Wild West shows, and Weadick and LaDue did both, according to what work was available.

During the golden age of vaudeville from 1900 to 1920, more than 25,000 "artists" delighted, bored and humoured audiences across the United States and Canada. Acts such as Amazon and Nile, contortionists; Buck and Bubbles, comedy act; Two Funny Sauerkrauts; the Dolly Twin Sisters; dog acts, Irish acts, high wire performers, singers, dancers, ropers, magicians— they all wove their short spells on audiences. Guy and Florence performed in vaudeville for nearly twenty years, from 1905 to the mid-1920s, picking up work in the winter months.

Vaudeville was demanding, exciting and gruelling. Guy, by poking around and asking questions, quickly learned what it took to arrange eighteen or nineteen acts into exact time slots, to pace the whole program so that the audience's attention was always "on," to promote a show before it arrived, to make complex and inexpensive travel arrangements and to put off angry artists demanding payment. Most of all, he learned what would sell and what was a "poor fish."

Vaudeville was billed as family entertainment, and Guy and Florence performed on the Keith-Albee circuit, often called the "Sunday School" circuit. Vaudeville was trying to break away from the more lurid reputation of burlesque by offering a program that even a preacher would enjoy. Each house— theatre, concert hall, small-town stage—posted its own rules of conduct, which artists disobeyed at their peril. For example, Boston did not permit the expression "as weak and helpless as a German mark"; in Pittsburgh, an act was ordered to substitute the word "dickens" for "devil" and to omit the line, "I've been studying abroad." And it was considered vulgar in Louisville to use the words "nightshirts" and "hot dog."

Free-Form Poetry

Trick and fancy roping were introduced to the United States by such great ropers as the Mexican Vincente Orapeza, who performed with Buffalo Bill's Wild West at the turn of the century. Orapeza's closing act was to spell his name in the air, one letter at a time, with a rope that seemed alive.

Fancy roping usually involves catching one or more horses by throwing a fancy loop or performing rope tricks from the back of an animal. Trick roping involves only the roper and the rope. It is loose-jointed, free-form poetry, full of humour and wit with a generosity of motion that is a delight to watch. A trick roper spins and twirls out a long rope into wedding rings, Texas skips, ocean waves, and vertical and horizontal loops.

The world of vaudeville was highly competitive, and whether they appeared as Weadick & LaDue or the Stampede Riders or Wild West Stunts, Guy and Florence had a small advantage over other performers. Because they performed with three bucking ponies and their small terrier, Bum, they needed the full stage. A full stage meant that the curtain had to close on their act, and the closing of a curtain always prompted applause.

Weadick and LaDue usually worked the small-time circuit: two different theatres a week, two to three performances a day, in a program that was usually five or six acts at most. They never played the Palace in New York, the mecca of all vaudevillians, but they were steadily employed. Weekly wages for acts at the time ranged from $75 to $3000 a week. A popular dog and pony act could earn $300 a week. Out of that, performers had to pay for their accommodation, meals, living expenses and travel.

Canada, with its cold weather and small theatres, was called "the Death Trail." Performances were given in Winnipeg, Regina, Moose Jaw, Saskatoon, Medicine Hat, Calgary, Edmonton and Vancouver. There were advantages, however, to the northern circuit. Prohibition was still in effect in the United States, but Canada wasn't yet "dry," and it warmed the heart of many a vaudevillian to see the fine array of whiskey on store shelves.

Guy and Florence honed their act over many miles and varied their patter to suit the location. They were popular performers and were frequently reviewed in local papers. In the flickering stage lights, dressed in his tall cowboy hat, Guy would start the patter. Tom Moore, writing in the *Albertan*, later recreated some of the dialogue:

> "Toughest trick is the Butterfly," Guy would say.
> "You start it like this—" and the rope would go into a knot.
> "So you start again like this—", another knot.
> "So you start again and try to reverse like this—", another knot.
> "In fact," he would wind up, "the durned thing is so tough it's impossible—" whereupon the loop would start doing figure eights in a perfect butterfly.

Weadick and LaDue also took their act to the Wild West circuit. More than a hundred Wild West shows, circuses and Wild West combinations,

The Vaudeville Circuit

For performers like Guy and Florence, vaudeville meant liberty and the chance to thrill new audiences every night. But it was also hard work. Veteran performer Ken Murray recalls the life: "It was rugged... and I still think of it in horror. The show would end at about eleven. At midnight, the railroad station's restaurant and most of the restaurants in town were closed. No dinner would be available on the train. Therefore, the performer sought out 'a little lunch place' [where he could] grab some sandwiches and bring 'em on the train. Though the vaudevillian may have eaten at six o'clock, it was six hours later, he had done a show and packed his trunks, and he was hungry. Since there usually were no lounge cars on the milk trains, the sandwiches would be eaten in the men's room. A good deal of the time the trains would be sidetracked and picked up several hours later that morning."

Indian congresses, travelling rodeos and concerts were active across North America between 1900 and 1916. The movie industry was also beginning to attract cowboy entertainers. But for most cowboys, the Wild West shows meant a chance to see some country. For top hands, it meant drawing sixty dollars a month, against forty a month on the range. Compared with the regular duties of a range hand, it seemed an easy life, travelling from one place to another and riding a bronc or two a day. But the Wild West show hand soon learned that much of his work came from the audience, who expected cowpunchers to look, act and dress in a certain way. Much of his time was spent answering questions about everything from Indian lore to chuckwagon recipes.

The big Wild West shows were actually small travelling communities, and the organization needed to put them together was truly impressive. The Miller Brothers 101 Ranch Wild West show was one of the most enduring and successful. It was able to draw performers from among 101 Ranch hands, whose skills were now recognized as being among the cream of the continent. By 1908, the Miller Brothers' show was travelling the country in its own forty-five-car railroad train.

The Miller brothers used part of their huge ranch as winter headquarters for the travelling show, and they employed a full range of specialists to maintain the operation. As Wild West veteran Milt Hinkle describes in *Frontier Times* magazine, "chandelier men" looked after the carbide lights; gold-leaf artists decorated the parade wagons; canvasmen made and repaired the tents; "Ammunition Shorty" reloaded shells for the blank shootings. A team of blacksmiths, harness makers, horse trainers, doctors, carpenters and ticket-takers made the show run. The publicity man was key. There were no radio stations, so he had to rely on newspapers, handbills and posters to reach the audiences. A special boiler was hauled on the train to cook and prepare the paste needed for billboards.

Perhaps the most thrilling and effective advertisement for the 101 Ranch Wild West was the traditional parade through town on opening day. Cowboys, cowgirls, Cossacks, Indians and Mexican vaqueros dressed in colourful costumes rode beautiful horses and waved to the tune of blaring music. Crowds followed them right to the grounds for a fast-paced program of twenty or more acts in the best Buffalo Bill tradition.

The Miller Brothers 101 Ranch Wild West would prove to be a perfect training ground for Guy Weadick. In spring 1908, he and Florence joined up with the show, which had just finished a popular performance at Madison Square Gardens in New York. The show was on a western Canadian swing, scheduled to appear in Calgary during the Dominion Exhibition. For Guy, it meant a chance to meet up with old friends and to join an outfit that would expand his experience and promotional skills. Florence enjoyed meeting other top cowgirls and studying their roping and riding skills.

The 101 Ranch Wild West arrived in Calgary in time to join the enormous parade that kicked off the exhibition on the morning of July 1, 1908. The famous 101 Ranch Wild West performers were greeted with cheers from the crowds who lined the way.

Calgary was growing rapidly from the western town Guy had first visited three years before. The exhibition pointed the way to the city's future. Calgary had been bitterly disappointed over the selection of Edmonton as the provincial capital three years earlier, and the further loss of the University of Alberta to the northern city still rankled. Everyone was determined to use the 1908 Dominion Exhibition to showcase the city to the country and the world. It was a formidable task. The entire province was recovering from the worst winter in years. Crops and livestock had been devastated, and there had been barely a year to prepare for the exhibition.

But the new exhibition manager, E. L. Richardson, was up to the task. Richardson had boundless optimism about the future of Calgary. Three years earlier, his essay on Calgary's bright future had been published by the Hundred Thousand Club, a group of city boosters whose goal was "to make Calgary the foremost city in the West, both commercially and industrially, to induce manufacturers and capitalists to locate here, and thus increase the population to 100,000." Ernie Richardson was a go-getter, an able administrator and an inspired organizer.

To launch the Dominion Exhibition, he organized special teams and committees and galvanized a formidable volunteer force. The program they came up with had something for everyone, including Richardson. An aviation enthusiast, he had arranged for Strobels' airship, a propeller-driven dirigible, to make three flights daily in front of the grandstand. A full program of vaudeville acts on the large central stage entertained the crowds, many of whom had been brought in by special excursion trains. By the time it was over on July 8, more than 100,000 people had enjoyed the exhibition.

The Miller Brothers Wild West show fit in with the enthusiasm of the time. An ad in the *Calgary Herald* proclaimed it to be "the only exposition of Western border life of its original kind and scope, by very nature and source impossible of duplication or imitation." The 101 Ranch offered a rich menu of western adventure, including "cowboys, vaqueros, senoritas, men and women sharpshooters, range riders, Pony Express Veterans, Bull Fighters, and all other real, actual, genuine, simon-pure denizens of the cow-camp and range, reproducing the Sports, Frolics, Games, Round-ups, Gallantries…and Romantic Daily Happenings of their lives. Everything except a Tenderfoot!"

Calgary was full of cowboys looking for fun and entrepreneurs cooking up schemes. Guy quickly made the rounds of the hotels and bars, getting reacquainted with old friends. He also spent time with H. C. McMullen, livestock agent for the Canadian Pacific Railway. Years before, McMullen had been associated with the cattle business in Wyoming, and he and Guy discovered they had mutual friends there. During one of their conversations, Guy wondered if Calgary might not be the city to host a frontier days celebration and championship cowboy contest on a big scale. It could, he thought, make a dandy annual event. The more he thought about it, the more he liked the idea. The celebration could include both a reunion of pioneers from all over the West and cowboy competitions for world championship titles and top prizes. It was a bold and ambitious scheme from a twenty-three-year-old. McMullen liked the proposal but was dubious about getting anyone to sponsor it financially. He and Guy parted with a handshake, agreeing to keep in touch.

Wherever he went, Guy naturally made his way to cowboy circles. In Lethbridge, he and Florence attended the southern Alberta riding and roping championships and participated with a roping performance of their own. Guy was pleased to learned that a large contingent of Blood people were on

In July 1908, Calgary welcomed the world to the Dominion Exhibition, showcasing western Canada as a land of exciting potential.

hand for the contest, and he was able to meet up with his old friend Crop-Eared Wolf, who was still wearing Guy's photo button.

That winter, Weadick and LaDue were back in vaudeville, performing with their horses and their roping tricks in the Broadway play "Billy the Kid." Later that winter, in Jacksonville, Florida, film director Sidney Olcott tried to sign them up to appear in a series of western pictures he was putting together. For Guy and Florence, it wasn't a difficult decision. The movie industry was uncertain at best, and they were show people who enjoyed the response of a live audience. Guy later said that he had seen too much of the genuine West and its people to be able to act out some of the scenes directors insisted were the real thing.

On February 23, 1911, Guy and Florence set sail with their horses on the L.S. *Laurentic* to Liverpool to take their act before European audiences.

Buffalo Bill's Wild West had whetted the European appetite for western performances, and with Guy's promotional skills, the couple had no trouble booking their act. They opened in Glasgow, Scotland, and from there went to London, performing at the Palladium, the Leicester Square Empire, the Palace and the Alhambra. Next they travelled to Europe, appearing at the Wintergarten in Berlin and other leading theatres in St. Petersburg, Moscow, Odessa, Vienna and Paris.

In Paris, Guy mentioned to the audience that he and Florence often used a lift or elevator to get their horses on stage and boasted that, if necessary, he could take his horse to the top of the Eiffel Tower. A lively international bet was laid, and permission was granted by French authorities to test the boast. Guy took his horse up three elevators to the top and won the bet. The wind and height unsettled Guy considerably, although his horse didn't mind a bit.

In another Paris incident, Guy offended French honour. On the way to the theatre, he had stopped for a shave and shampoo and been grossly over-charged. He couldn't argue the matter in French, but he took it out on the barber that night on stage, mimicking the man's actions and saying that he was a worse robber than any of the bandits of the Old West. The bit went over well with the largely English and American audience.

The French, he thought, had appreciated the humour as well, for they sent

Guy Weadick knew the importance of publicity and wasn't afraid of startling passersby. In Paris he took his horse and Stetson to the boulevard to promote his act.

a special delegation to his dressing room after the show, gesturing and talking about "satisfaction." Guy nodded and smiled and tried to indicate he was happy they were satisfied with his show. Finally he enlisted the translation skills of a French theatre attendant who could speak some English, and it soon became clear that the French men had not enjoyed the show at all. They were there to defend the honour of their friend, the barber. A duel to the death was the "satisfaction" they were seeking.

As the challenged party, Guy was given the choice of weapons. In true western tradition, he suggested the lariat. Failing that, he offered to knock the barber into the middle of next week. The group was outraged at this ungentlemanly suggestion and an uproar ensued. Guy finally shooed everyone out and made his way home.

At times Guy and Florence seemed far from the western landscape of the true cowboy, but they were spreading the cowboy's story, and they were excited by the response they were receiving.

Throughout his life, Guy adopted the pose and costume of the cowboy of stage and popular literature. He became a walking, talking advertisement for the cowboy spirit.

The Selling of a Stampede

WHILE GUY AND FLORENCE were performing on stages throughout the United States and Europe, Calgary was going through a boom that was transforming it from a frontier town into a thriving western city. The same railroad cars that had been used to ship cattle were now bringing in a more exciting, profitable load—settlers, farmers, businesspeople and entrepreneurs eager to try their hand at the opportunities promised in the "Last Best West" of the federal immigration posters. Building permits skyrocketed to $62,747,000 in 1911, and the population had doubled to 50,000 since the 1908 Dominion Exhibition. The Canadian Pacific Railway had expanded its shops and yards to a new complex in the Ogden area of the city to accommodate the increased shipping. An impressive new

4

livestock and horse show arena, with seating for 3,000, had been built on the Exhibition Grounds.

Calgary was looking ahead to a bright future as the centre for commerce and industry in the western prairies. It also made sense to diversify. The ranching and agricultural industry surrounding the city was changing. Over a series of bad winters, local ranchers had learned the bitter lesson that cattle could not survive on open ranges during killing blizzards. After suffering tremendous losses during these years, ranchers had begun to keep their cattle closer to home, feeding them on home-grown hay. And government-leased land that had previously been used for ranching was being sold off to settlers who were more interested in farming. The traditional life of the cowboy was changing.

The cowboy was seen as a bit of a hooligan in Calgary. Newspapers reported an incident where spurred and chapped horsemen shot at an automobiling party before riding away, laughing, into the night. In another incident, a bank robber's hideaway was found strewn with cowboy trappings, including lurid western novels. Reports from as far away as Paris indicated that cowboys were influencing the wilder side of society. Apache dances were the rage of bohemian Paris, and a rash of European robberies was attributed to the influence of cowboy thrillers.

H. C. McMullen was watching the growth of the city and remembering his conversation with the enthusiastic young cowboy Guy Weadick three years before. McMullen noticed that small one-day rodeos were becoming popular throughout cattle country. Cowboys enjoyed testing their skills, and crowds were gathering to watch them. There was a land boom going on in western Canada, supported by the federal government, the railway and the land companies. World-wide publicity was attracting settlers to the advantages of the Canadian northwest. McMullen wrote to Guy in Europe, suggesting they get together to pursue the proposal for a frontier days event.

Guy and Florence arrived in Calgary in March 1912, accompanied by Tom Mix, who was waiting to take over as arena director with a new Wild West show that Col. Fred T. Cummins was launching on a U.S. tour. Guy had been offered the job but had turned it down, seeing greater opportunity in the

Manager of the Calgary Exhibition and Stampede for thirty-nine years, Ernie Richardson paid careful attention to finances and administrative details, providing a strong balance to Weadick's promotional skills.

foothills, nearer to the true cowboy life he loved. Guy and Florence were broke, and Guy was gambling on the letter from McMullen.

Together, the two men sketched out a week-long program for a "Frontier Days and Cowboy Championship Contest." As Guy had suggested initially, it was to be a reunion of western pioneers and a celebration of the cowboys, ranchers and old-timers who had shaped the West. "There will be," Guy promised, "no representations of old time criminality such as robbing stage coaches, etc. The affair will not be a wild west show." They would call it a "stampede," a name that hadn't been used before, and they were sure it would out-draw similar events at Pendleton or Cheyenne. There was just one hitch: they were going to have to drum up $100,000 to make it work.

Guy and McMullen began canvassing the Calgary business community for support, but the response was discouraging. Most thought the idea was simply too big for Calgary. Besides, the day of the cowboy was over, they said. Wheat was King. Alberta was looking ahead. Business meant progress, and ranching was a thing of the past.

Guy approached Ernie Richardson, now manager of the Calgary Industrial Exhibition Company, to see if the Exhibition Grounds could be rented for the western celebration. Richardson was polite but busy. The grounds were the site of year-long activity: livestock shows, exhibitions, horse auctions, specialty stock shows and other events. Richardson didn't have time for old-time reunions, and his response to Guy was a flat no.

It began to seem as if the idea would never be more than a dream. However, Tom Mix had stopped briefly to find work with Ad Day on the Big Horse Ranch, south of Medicine Hat. Mix mentioned the stampede idea to Day, who owned a string of bucking horses and had produced several local competitions. Day came up to Calgary to find out if there was a possibility of adapting the idea for Medicine Hat.

He joined McMullen and Guy at the Alberta Hotel, and they talked over the idea. The proposal was good, Day thought, but too rich for Medicine Hat. Nonetheless, he offered to put up $10,000 in cash and supply all his top horses and other stock needed for the show if Guy could come up with the financial sponsorship in Calgary.

Unlikely Partners

As James H. Gray points out in an article in *Citymakers,* Guy Weadick and Ernie Richardson were an unusual team. "Weadick was basketballer-thin, over six feet tall. Richardson was undersized and plump. Weadick was a fun-loving hedonist, Richardson a devout Christian Scientist and family man. Weadick was a 'two-fisted drinking man,' while Richardson drank nothing stronger than tea. Richardson's tastes and enthusiasm encompassed the entire field of entertainment, and Weadick's were confined to cowboying. The bottom line was always a factor in Richardson's decision making; for Weadick the show was the thing, the costs always secondary."

As Guy entered the Alberta Hotel the next morning, he was approached by Aleck Fleming, manager of the Bar U Ranch. Fleming's boss, George Lane, wanted to talk to Guy about his Frontier Days idea. The young entrepreneur and the seasoned cowman met in Lane's room for the next couple of hours. Lane asked Guy to return that afternoon to discuss the plan further, and he invited wealthy ranchers Pat Burns and A. E. Cross to join them. It was a charged, historic meeting. The four men agreed that the celebration would recreate the atmosphere of the frontier West in an authentic manner, "devoid of circus tinsel and far fetched fiction." It was to blend a reunion of truly western pioneers and their families with competitions that would showcase the work of cowboys on the range. The three ranchers delivered their instructions to Guy over a handshake: "Make it the best thing of its kind in the world—but everything must be on the square. We don't want to lose money if we can help it, but we'd rather lose money and have it right than make money and have it wrong."

The next day, Lane, Burns and Cross met with the Exhibition Board directors and arranged for the use of the Exhibition Grounds at Victoria Park. They then took Guy to the bank, where they informed the manager they were opening an account of $100,000 in the name of a Frontier Days Celebration Committee. Each of the men contributed $25,000, and they guaranteed a further $25,000 from Archie McLean, another Alberta ranchman who was provincial secretary in the Alberta government at the time.

The endorsement of Lane, Burns, Cross and McLean, who soon became known as "the Big Four," went a long way. These were men who had taken risks of their own, who had seen personal visions fulfilled through hard work. In Guy's Frontier Days proposal, they recognized something of their own energy and vision. With their support, Weadick and McMullen had all they needed.

An agreement was made with Ad Day to use his bucking horses, saddle stock and pickup men for a percentage of the profits. Day was also appointed arena director. Ernie Richardson was appointed treasurer in charge of financial arrangements for the event. H. C. McMullen, as the official director general, began organizing the most impressive parade the West had ever seen.

Guy became general manager, with duties to "manage, produce, and publicize the event." A stampede committee with George Lane as chairman was established, and the group swung into action.

You can't run a cow outfit on conversation, Guy once said, but at a time when newspapers didn't reach into remote cow camps, before radio and television, he knew the value of word of mouth and how to pass the word along. The "GW" on his belt buckle, he laughingly said, stood for "Good with Words."

The stampede was set for September 2, 3, 4 and 5. The timing of the event was difficult. It had to be long enough after harvesting for ranchers and farmers to attend, yet close enough in time to other western events that good bucking stock could be brought to Calgary.

Guy knew the drawing power of celebrities, and when it was announced that the Duke of Connaught, who was then the Governor General of Canada, was to be in Calgary along with his wife and his popular daughter Princess Patricia during the week of the stampede, Guy fired off an invitation to them, increased the run of the show from four to six days to accommodate them,

The Big Four

George Lane, Alfred Ernest Cross, Pat Burns and Archie McLean, the original backers of the Calgary Stampede, were four of the most powerful men in ranch country. Lane was a former American cavalry scout and cowboy who came to Alberta from Montana in 1884 to be the foreman of the massive Bar U Ranch at Pekisko. Eventually he bought the Bar U. Cross was the son of a prominent Montreal judge. He had also arrived in Calgary in 1884. A graduate of the Ontario Agricultural College, Cross owned the impressive A7 Ranch near Nanton, the Calgary Brewery and other businesses. Burns, an Irish immigrant, worked his way west from Manitoba by supplying beef for the railroad. Once he reached Calgary, he diversified into beef slaughter and processing, and by 1912 he was a millionaire. McLean had come west from Ontario in 1886, cowpunched for a while and then become managing partner of the CY, or Cypress Cattle Company, near Taber. In 1909, he became a minister in the Alberta provincial government.

The historic meeting between Weadick and the Big Four was recreated in a popular diorama at the Horseman's Hall of Fame in Calgary.

and ordered two special royal boxes built across from the grandstand. He wanted to invite King George V, too, but was stalled by the committee.

Two hundred head of Mexican steers were brought in from the Blood reserve south of Calgary for roping and dogging. Wild steers belonging to George Lane were also sent to Calgary. Ad Day shipped two hundred horses as bucking stock and wild horses. Johnny Mullens, a cowboy showman, was put in charge of the rodeo stock.

Details were quickly hammered out. Bleachers sprang up around the race track at Victoria Park. Reserved seating in the grandstand would cost fifty cents above the gate admission of a dollar. Sandwiches and ice cream cones would be ten cents each. There was to be no carnival or midway; the stampede was the sole attraction.

Guy had learned the lessons of good advertising from the 101 Ranch Wild West show and the vaudeville circuit, where timing was key. He waited until the Exhibition was in full swing in June, with readers eagerly watching the daily reports from the fair in the newspapers, then broke the story of "The Stampede, a Reunion of Old Timers in the Great West," with a full-page black-lettering announcement.

From then on, no one could escape the news of the coming stampede. Guy placed a series of attractive, showy ads in all the papers. In one, using a drawing by the well-known western artist Ed Borein as an illustration, he heralded the coming of champion cowboys and cowgirls from the Cheyenne Frontier Days, the Pendleton Round-up and "all the leading Wild West Shows and…every cattle district in Mexico, the United States and Canada." If readers didn't completely understand what a stampede was, they were soon caught up in the excitement anyway.

On a visit to Cheyenne Frontier Days in Wyoming, Guy saw a good audience for his stampede. "We're going to have some show up there," he told them. "We're going to spread the history of the great northwest before our visitors so they can see in an hour or two what it takes students years to learn, and we're going to show them what a genuine contest— every letter a capital—really is."

Guy's message combined braggadocio with nostalgia. He challenged west-

The first Stampede paid warm tribute to the Big Four ranchers and provided a guide for visitors to the exciting schedule of competitions.

erners and appealed to their sentimentality. "While this is to be a season of joy, a period rich in reminiscences, an occasion of hearty greetings, and renewal of old friendships," he said, "there will be just a tinge of sadness as we gaze upon the 'sunset of a dying race'." On the other hand, as he wrote in the promotional brochure, the Frontier Days Celebration and Stampede would be "entertainment on such a grand scale of magnificence as would be a fitting finale to the glorious history of the justly celebrated range."

Guy reached into the far corners of cow country, north and south, with news of the upcoming stampede. It was a western event, but he invited the world. He recalled every contact, every chance conversation, every influential name he had come across in five years of touring North America and Europe. He fired off letters, telegrams and entry forms to cowboys and cowgirls, entertainers, royalty, Mexican vaqueros, musicians, writers and western artists—anyone who would carry the message of the stampede received a personal letter. His combination of enthusiasm and thoroughness proved irresistible, and top-notch performers began to respond positively.

Guy wanted to reward the stampede competitors in a way they would fully appreciate and talk about. Twenty thousand dollars in gold, along with world championship titles and many other valuable prizes were offered—five times the value of any prizes that had been offered anywhere in the world up to that time. Since there was no regulation or official organization, world championships were frequently offered at rodeos and frontier events. But titles won at the larger rodeos such as the Cheyenne Frontier Days and the Pendleton Roundup carried much more weight because the top performers all attended. The Calgary Stampede promised a competition that would outclass them all.

Like any good vaudeville theatre manager, Guy understood the importance of staging side events that would contribute to the overall excitement of the main program. Recalling the Sun Dance ceremony he had witnessed in 1904, Guy invited hundreds of First Nations peoples from all over Alberta to attend the stampede, encouraging them to wear full ceremonial dress. The aging Methodist missionary Rev. John McDougall of nearby Morley was deputized for a fee of $390 to gather representatives from the aboriginal peoples together for the event.

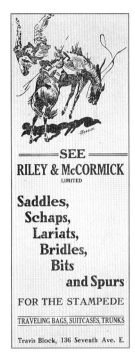

Local businesses backed the Stampede with advertising, special prices and competition prizes. Many decorated their windows with western displays and banners.

But it was uncertain at first whether the government would "allow" First Nations people to participate. Although they had been an important part of summer fairs and holiday events since the 1890s, by 1900 the government was trying to turn native people into farmers and ranchers. Attendance at fairs was counterproductive to that goal, said the officials, and they were backed by the moral reform leagues and the churches.

Weadick and McMullen, however, saw the native presence as key to the stampede's success. They pulled considerable strings, from the mayor of Calgary to Senator James Lougheed and Member of Parliament R. B. Bennett. Less than a month before the stampede opened, the government backed down, and some 2,000 aboriginal people attended the stampede, set up tipis near the replica of a Hudson's Bay Company post, presented daily dances and competed in the events.

As another side event, Guy called on his cowboy artist friends Charlie Russell and Ed Borein to exhibit their work and persuaded them to create some promotional art for the stampede. A display of their work on the grounds would turn out to be one of the highlights of the week-long program.

Despite its initial misgivings, the Exhibition Board threw its enthusiasm, support and considerable experience into making the stampede a success. Key to this cooperation was the role of Ernie Richardson. In the months before the first stampede, Guy and "E. L." forged a working relationship that was to last for the next twenty years.

Tickets for the great event went on sale on August 5 and were quickly snapped up, despite some grumbling about the high entry fee as compared to the twenty-five-cent admission charged for the Exhibition. The stampede promised to be a special event, however, and no one wanted to miss it. By August 17 Guy announced that advance sales had reached $20,000.

There were no highways in 1912 and very few automobiles, but visitors from across the country began to arrive on horseback, by buckboard and wagon, and on foot. The Canadian Pacific Railway offered special stampede trains, and an estimated 40,000 passengers took advantage of the half-fare excursion rate from as far away as Winnipeg. Every hotel in the city was booked, and restaurants did a thriving trade. Half a dozen Pinkerton detectives were brought in to foil pickpockets and confidence men. Once the hotels were full, tent cities sprang up on riverbanks and in vacant lots. A replica of the famous Fort Whoop-Up, the centre of the whiskey trade, was built on the grounds, with whiskey trader Fred Kanouse on hand to reminisce with old friends.

The whole city of Calgary went western. Businesses and private residences were decorated with ribbon and bunting. Competitors were required to "dress western" at all times, and everyone appeared in their best western finery.

But it wasn't all show by any means. Guy was adamant that the stampede would be a true cowboy contest, not a dressed-up exhibition match. He wanted working cowboys to meet and compete and be recognized for their role in the development of the West. And he didn't want the event to be the last hurrah for the western cowboy, either. In the program copy, he planted the idea of continuing the stampede on an annual basis and asked readers to let him know what they thought.

The stage was set for the biggest extravaganza the West had ever seen.

Flores LaDue took the title of Lady Champion Fancy Roper at the first Calgary Stampede. Although only five feet tall, she was able to rope a galloping horse and rider from a standing position.

The Real Thing and a Whole Lot of It

THE FIRST CALGARY STAMPEDE kicked off on Labour Day, Monday, September 2, 1912, with the "greatest pioneer pageant that ever traversed a city's street." Calgary's population of 40,000, swollen to 60,000 for the event, lined the streets to watch history unfold.

Leading the way were the First Peoples of the plains and the foothills. Nearly 2,000 Blood, Sarcee and Blackfoot people, dressed in beaded clothing, feathered headdresses, paint and buffalo hides, along with painted ponies, were greeted with appreciation by the crowds.

They were followed by a contingent representing the pioneer missionaries who had brought the gospel to the West. Hudson's Bay Company factors and traders, Red River carts, whiskey traders and veterans of the original North-

West Mounted Police dressed in the costume of their day made a colourful showing, as did pioneer cowmen and ranch owners with chuckwagons. Frontier stagecoaches driven by men who had carried the Royal mail, bullwhackers with their long strings of yoke oxen, prairie schooners, and pioneer settlers and their families all contributed to the pageantry.

Following these groups came the competitors: hundreds of mounted cowboys and cowgirls from all over Canadian and American range country, waving and prancing, ready for the various thrilling events that made up the program.

A section of the parade devoted to the industrial progress of the West featured labour union members, craftspeople and colourful floats paying tribute to business. The Trade and Labour Council was a hasty addition; they had intended to hold their own procession on Labour Day but accepted a $1,500 bribe to join the parade peaceably. Pointing the way to the future were floats of Calgary schoolchildren, boys and girls who would be the leaders of tomorrow. The music of the Pendleton Mounted Band filled the air.

Parade audiences got some unscheduled reminders of the Old West, too. Phil Weinard, a pioneer citizen of High River, western performer and close friend of Charlie Russell's, was driving an impressive eight yoke of big steers in the parade. As Bert Sheppard recalls in his book *Spitzee Days*, "This outfit was a great attraction, and many were awed by the bullwhacker's skill in cracking his great whip. These whips were so long and so heavy that it took both hands to wield one. On the narrow streets he had to drag it behind him before cracking it, in order to avoid hitting spectators. At one point along the route a horse following the freight wagons stepped on the whip just as Phil gave it a mighty heave to snap it forward. The whip didn't move but Phil did. He hit the pavement flat on his back. Spectators within ear-shot got a much more authentic impression of a bullwhacker in action than the Stampede Committee bargained for."

The crowds followed the parade down to the Exhibition Grounds. In the best Wild West tradition, the stampede began with the grand entry of all the mounted riders, who galloped around the track as they were presented to the audience.

THE PENDLETON BAND
THE STAMPEDE "CALGARY ALTA 1912

There had never been such an impressive show of events—seventeen in all, with more than 150 contestants and respected judges from among the finest cowmen in the country. Archie McLean and George Lane lent their experience, as did Herb Miller and Aleck Fleming from the Bar U. No one was sure how long it would take to complete each event or what special problems might spring up. The general rules for the competitions were just that— general. Rule number 5 made that clear: "The management reserves the right to make any additional rules that circumstances may demand to govern any event." Canadian cowboy Clem Gardner later recalled the confusion that resulted: "The various technicalities, explained to contestants the day before the big show opened, were to prove quite a problem to new contestants, unused to them. Some of us were 'green' and unknown to the judges and their decisions often floored us."

Pendleton, Oregon, had been hosting an annual Frontier Days since 1888, and for the Calgary Stampede, they sent the Pendleton Mounted Band to play in the parade.

The line-up of events, identical each day, provided the diversion and rhythm of a good vaudeville program. In showbiz terms, it was a good sell— warming the audience up with some fancy trick riding by cowgirls, following that with a "big act," the stagecoach ride, and balancing out the rest of the program with the thrills and danger and dexterity of bucking bronco riding, steer bulldogging and roping. Each day ended with a wild free-for-all.

The performers and the audience were blessed with sunny skies on opening day, but the next few days were marred by cloudy skies and showers. On Thursday, the day of the vice-regal appearance, a heavy thunderstorm turned the centre field into a slippery, muddy mess. The show was quickly moved to the new horse-show arena, and thousands scrambled for seats, with many having to be turned away.

The weather may have been an inconvenience for onlookers, but it made tough work for rodeo contestants. "To give an idea of how wet and greasy the ground was—during the roping contest my horse went down just as I threw my steer and was still down when the steer was tied," Clem Gardner recalled. And when a few flakes of snow drifted down with the rain, a disgusted American cowpuncher complained, "Boy, I've already bought me a raincoat up here, and I don't want to have to get a fur one too."

The events themselves were long on promotion and short on delivery, but no one really minded. Umbrellas sprang up, and rain and uncomfortable seats were ignored in the excitement of the competition. Most events went on far too long, with unexplained delays. There were no chutes for the bucking stock, so the broncs had to be blindfolded or even hobbled while the cowboy or cowgirl quickly climbed on for a ride that had no time limit. The steers brought in for the steer roping proved too fast for the Canadian rope horses and had to be chased as much as a quarter of a mile. Competitors often found themselves at the far end of the vast centre field, far from the view of the audience.

A pall was cast over the events by the death of Joe LaMar, a popular Alberta bronc rider, who had been killed a few days before the opening of the stampede while trying out bucking horses in the enclosed evening arena. Red Wing, the big Medicine Hat sorrel he was riding, fell down while bucking, catching LaMar's new chap belt over the saddle horn. LaMar was

Guy poses with the chiefs of the Stoneys, Sarcees and Blackfoot at the first Stampede. Despite government officials' initial reluctance, the First Nations people made an impressive presence at this and subsequent stampedes.

severely kicked before they could get him free. He died on the way to the hospital, and the incident sparked an outcry about the brutality of the sport. The stampede management organized a benefit performance one evening and gave the gate receipts, more than $2,000, to LaMar's widow. One of the highlights of the benefit performance was the final event, in which Goldie St. Clair, an experienced American bucking horse rider, successfully rode Red Wing before a breathless crowd.

Among the other female competitors at the Calgary Stampede were Florence LaDue, trick roper; Dolly Mullens, trick rider; bronc riders Bertha

Blancett, Fanny Sperry, Hazel Walker and Annie Schaffer; and Lucille Mulhall, the only female steer roper. On the final day, Fanny Sperry rode slick on Red Wing. It was a thrilling ride that left the audience gasping, especially Fanny's mother, who was watching from the royal box. When the hazer finally pulled her off, Fanny bowed and waved. She had won the title of Lady Bucking Horse Champion of the World. The skill and bold riding of the cowgirl competitors delighted audiences, and the local newspapers gave them full coverage.

Excitement grew as the week progressed and both the crowds and the contestants came to understand the events better. The Canadian competitors were up against some formidable American riders: Joe Gardner, Harry Webb, Tex Macleod, Eddie "Doc" Pardee, Art Accord and Charles Tipton had already honed their skills and reputations in American rodeos and Wild West shows. The Calgary audiences became discouraged as prize after prize went south of the border. But the stampede was truly an international event, an opportunity to witness the talents of outstanding riders and performers from all over North America.

Without chutes and an infield arena, events such as steer roping often wandered far from the grandstand audiences.

With the outlaw horse Cyclone, Tom Three Persons drew the ride of his life, but he held on to win the title of World Champion Bucking Horse Rider.

The horses that had been brought in for the events soon became as legendary as the contestants. Three renowned bucking horses, Gaviota, Tornado and Cyclone, were challenging the best riders in the world and offering tough odds. The two blacks, Cyclone and Gaviota, were fast, salty and wild. They were owned by Del and Bertha Blancett, experienced performers from Oklahoma, who had shipped the horses to Calgary especially for the stampede.

Cyclone was an outlaw who had tossed 127 riders over seven years, and at the Stampede he quickly became known as the "unrideable Black Demon" or the "Black Terror." The horse had to be thrown down and saddled on the ground, because if he was saddled standing he would throw himself backwards. Once the rider was positioned over the animal with his feet in the stirrups, the handlers would let the horse up. There was no chance for a rider to settle himself into the saddle. Cyclone also had the trick of rearing, giving the impression that he was going right over, then coming down.

The sight of Cyclone's explosive bucking was alarming, even for experienced riders. It especially unnerved the tall young cowboy who would ride him in the final bucking competition. Tom Three Persons was a twenty-five-year-old Blood who had been bailed out of a Fort Macleod jail where he was resting after indulging in too much pre-Stampede spirit. Indian Agent Glen Campbell had rushed him up to Calgary to compete, and Three Persons had performed well. On Saturday, however, he drew the ride of his life. He had seen the big black dash riders to the ground all week; he had never encountered such a horse, and he asked veteran bronc rider Rod Redfern for advice. Redfern could only shake his head and warn Three Persons to watch the horse's rearing and be ready when the horse came down.

It was a breathless ride. Cyclone performed one ferocious leap after another, pitching, rearing, bucking from one end of the grounds to the other. But when the dust settled, Tom Three Persons was still on his back. He was the new World Champion Bucking Horse Rider. The crowd went wild, cheering, throwing hats in the air and yelling the new word they had discovered: "Whoooopee!"

Three Persons later recalled the ride in a conversation with Alberta newspaperman Fred Kennedy: "Cyclone wasn't too tough when he was buckin'

Range skills were put to the test as cowboys competed to rope and ride wild horses in record time.

FIGHTING WILL

AT THE STAMPED

OFFICIAL PHOTO No 87.
MARCELL OF CALGARY

straight ahead. But when he sucked back and started to raise in front, he could balance on one hind leg better'n any bronc I had ever seen. Well he starts to raise with me after the fifth jump, and scared the hell right out of me. I thought he was coming over backwards. Without realizing what I was really doin', I started to beller at him. He was so surprised that he flattened out. I knew I had 'im then so I just kept on spurring until I heard the whistle. The thing that I can remember best about that ride, was that the band kept playing the same tune over and over and people kept singing. I asked Guy Weadick what they were singing. He said, 'There will be a hot time in the old town tonight.' And there sure as hell was."

Canadians made a good showing in the final count. Because of the confusion over judging technicalities, Clem Gardner was surprised and pleased to find that he had won the All-Around Champion Cowboy award, which netted him $1,000. Florence LaDue took the honours in the Cowgirl's Fancy Roping category.

By most accounts the stampede was a rip-snorting success. The vice-regal party, along with many friends who had come out from England for the celebration, had had a wonderful time. The show had played to more than 100,000 admissions and grossed more than $120,000. After all expenses were paid, it disbursed $3,100 to Guy Weadick, in addition to the $425 he was paid in salary and a special silver mounted saddle; $4,000 to H. C. McMullen and $5,000 to Ad Day. The Big Four had promised from the beginning that if there was any profit from the stampede, they would donate their share to local charities. There was no profit, but Burns, Lane and Cross made donations anyway, to the General and Holy Cross hospitals and the Victorian Order of Nurses.

Guy, remembering the National Editorial Convention at the 101 Ranch, made sure that the stampede was fully covered by members of the Canadian, United States and British press. They were given every opportunity to photograph, interview and record the full story. Moving pictures were just emerging—a newsreel of the 1909 Exhibition pageant had been produced as part of a Canadian Pacific Railway promotional film—and the 1912 parade and stampede were also captured on this new medium.

Bertha Blancett was one of the successful participants in the 1912 Stampede's Ladies' Relay Race.

The event got a mixed review in the local newspapers. The *Herald* applauded the generosity and vision of the Big Four and the stampede management but condemned the faulty organization, which had sometimes turned crowds away with only minimal entertainment and expensive programs. The *Calgary News-Telegram* agreed, calling for the stampede as an annual event but suggesting that "a man of the ability of Ernie Richardson, secretary-treasurer and manager of the Exhibition company, should be secured as manager of the Stampede." Hinting at an "easy money fraternity," the *News-Telegram* editorialized that the irritating delays during competitions "were entirely due to one man and just why the 'Big Four' should have allowed him to interfere with the pleasure of forty to fifty thousand patrons we cannot understand."

For Guy, the most gratifying response came from his old friend western artist Charlie Russell, who spoke to Guy's heartfelt wish that the Stampede be recognized by old-timers as a true western competition. The following letter appears in Russell's book *Good Medicine*.

> Friend Guy:…Iv seen some roping an riding but never before have I seen so much of it bunched as I did at Calgary Ive seen some good wild west showes but I wouldent call what you pulled off a show. it was the real thing an a whole lot of it
>
> those horses judging from the way they unloded them twisters wasent broke for gramdas pheaton, they were shure snakey an your cattel dident act like dary stock to me I dont think aney I saw had been handled by milk maids. they were shure a supprise to those old cow poneys that had been runing short horns all there life. It wasent hardly fair to spring a gray hound waring horns an Guy football ain't so gentl—the bull ring an prise fighting is some rough but bull doging those long horns makes all other dangerous sports look like nursery games
>
> I am not alone in my praise of the Stampede. there are other men better judges than myself make the same talk.

Tillie Baldwin, wearing her distinctive riding bloomers, leads the way in the breathtaking Roman Races at the Winnipeg Stampede.

On the Road Again

6

GUY WAS JUBILANT at pulling off his dream, and he was eager to put his promotional skills to work again. Although he and Florence had made many new friends in Calgary, it was time to move on. The city was appreciative but not yet ready to make the stampede an annual event.

The Big Four had fulfilled their commitment, and they offered up the reins to anyone who wanted to take on the event. The lines were picked up in Winnipeg, where James Ryan Sr. and W. H. Fares joined forces with Ad Day in inviting Guy to stage a second stampede. Winnipeg wasn't a cowboy town, but it was in the midst of a real estate boom and ambitious for new businesses and land buyers. The organizers wanted to pull off a big event to draw attention to the city.

The dates for the Winnipeg Stampede were set as August 9 to 13, 1913. Half-fare railway rates were again offered, and Winnipeg businessmen rubbed their hands together at the prospect of more than 60,000 people roaming the streets for a week. Tickets at the gate would be one dollar, with an extra fifty-cent charge for reserved seats.

Guy set out to build excitement the same way he had in Calgary. Newspapers were bombarded with articles, advertising and announcements heralding the arrival of the stampede. A striking Ed Borein drawing of three whooping cowboys thundered across an ad that promised the event would make Winnipeg "the Mecca of America" and be "a Glorious, Gorgeous Gala Week for the West! The Whirlwind that Draws the World to Winnipeg! Life's Supreme Sensational Thrill to the Tenderfoot! The Royal Tournament of the Passing Range."

Gone was the nostalgia for the dying West; in its place was showbiz hucksterism at its most lurid: "The Great Arena will Fill with its circle of Throbbing Life. Then—the blare of a trumpet, the silken swirling sibilant swish of loosened lariat and the thud of a thousand hoofs—Stampede will be on!"

In one large ad, a hand-drawn map of North America, with Winnipeg at the centre, showed trains converging on the stampede from Kansas City, Chicago, Toronto, Montreal, San Francisco and Calgary, steamboats plying their way from Europe and businessmen walking from the East Coast yelling, "Me for that Stampede Thing." Over it all was the smiling modest face of Guy Weadick saying, "I think there'll be a Crowd."

As it had been in Calgary, the purse was $20,000. An arena was laid out inside the half-mile racetrack at the Winnipeg Exhibition Grounds, and a long surrounding row of bleachers was erected to augment the limited seating capacity of the grandstand. Local firms and the press were enthusiastically cooperative, and large groups of citizens were on the grounds daily to watch the work and the arrival of the stock, the cowboys and the cowgirls. Louis W. Hill, chairman of the board of directors of the Great Northern Railway, announced to the press, "The Stampede at Winnipeg, Canada, will be the biggest event on the American continent in 1913, and will be the greatest advertisement the Canadian northwest has ever had."

Winnipeg Says "Welcome"

Guy's ads for the Winnipeg Stampede reached new heights of promotional enthusiasm. This one filled a full page in the *Winnipeg Tribune*: "The Lid is Off—Stampede! In the presence of such a gorgeous prodigality of sensation and tireless thrill—language fails, words blow up! The previously punctureless and proud poise of the prince of press agents falls back from the Spectacle of the Supreme Stampede and gibbering takes the count? Twenty Carloads of Cayuses that can buck the corners off the stars. Everybody here from Everywhere. Women! You'd wonder where they came from—Champions—and ropers—rough riders—An' all good lookin! Palefaces!—Thousands and thousands of them—from Everywhere; come to Winnipeg—the town that knows how to say 'Welcome.'"

Trick Riding

One of the most popular—and dangerous—acts presented at the Winnipeg Stampede was that of two earnest young riders seeking to emulate the great Otto Kline, then the World's Champion Trick Rider. Boy Day, son of Ad Day, and his friend Pete Sanderson, had developed a novelty act in which both boys worked the same horse at the same time. As the horse galloped down the track at full speed, Boy Day would stand erect in the saddle with his hands high in the air, while Sanderson did a back-drag, his hands picking up gravel and throwing it in the air as he hung head down. The act won tremendous applause and gasps of astonishment from both the crowds and the professional trick riders watching the event.

Once again, Guy remained loyal to his ambition for a true cowboy contest. In an ad in the *Winnipeg Tribune*, he pointed out emphatically that "The Stampede is positively not affiliated or connected with any Wild West Show or combination of shows. It is an open challenge event for the largest cash prizes ever given anywhere, open to all comers." Working rodeo cowboys turned out in force for the Winnipeg event, attracted by the prizes and the fun that had been delivered to them in Calgary. They weren't disappointed.

Guy put together an exciting program for his second stampede. Chuckwagons, which would later become the star event at the Calgary Stampede, had not yet made their appearance on the racetrack, although Cheyenne Frontier Days had featured a "roundup race" using chuckwagons

in 1905. Guy arranged for a genuine range chuckwagon to be brought to Winnipeg with a real roundup cook in charge. This was where all the cowboys working on stock and chutes were fed.

The cowgirls once again drew media attention. Reporters were amused and intrigued to report that the top "cowboy" steer roper during the week was a cowgirl, Lucille Mulhall. Florence again won the title of World Champion Cowgirl Trick Roper. Overall, the lineup of events was basically the same as in Calgary, but the organizers had learned from their previous Calgary experiences and the Winnipeg show was better run. All event winners were awarded gold medals along with their cash winnings.

Gross receipts for the five-day cowboy contest reportedly amounted to $210,000. Expenditures came to approximately $100,000. Management cleared about $50,000.

By 1914, Guy and Florence were back in New York City, opening at Madison Square Gardens with the 101 Ranch Wild West. Florence, with her trick roping and her world titles, was a featured attraction. Guy's promotional skills were now more in demand than his roping tricks, and he was contracted as Joe Miller's personal representative to handle public relations for a show Miller was sending to England. Half of the 101 Show remained in the United States, touring the regular circuit, while the other half, with Zack Miller, went to London. The London show featured the reigning stars of the Wild West business: Guy and Florence, trick ropers Chester Byers and Hank Durnell, sharpshooter Stack Lee, cowgirl ropers and riders Alice Lee and Mabel Clive, and a large group of Sioux performers. Bill Pickett's bulldogging act was the headline attraction.

The show opened in late May at the Anglo-American Exposition in Shepherd's Bush Stadium. There were two ninety-minute shows each day, and the Wild West played for six months to record crowds that included many distinguished guests. Through London aristocrat Lord Lonsdale, Guy invited Queen Alexandria and her sister, the Empress Marie of Russia, to attend the show, as well as the Princess Royal and Princess Maude, the prime minister of Australia and many other notables, including the Duke of Connaught, who all enjoyed the spirited performances.

Eager to start a tradition, Guy promoted the stampede in Winnipeg as Canada's second annual frontier days celebration.

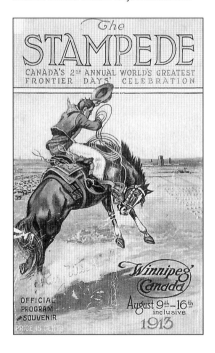

Lucille Mulhall, popularly called the first cowgirl, was a champion lady steer roper.

As before, his European travels provided rich story material for Guy. One of the most amusing anecdotes involved Lord Lonsdale, an accomplished rider himself, who had become friendly with the 101 Ranch performers and asked Guy if there were anything he could do to make their stay in London really memorable. Guy replied that they would enjoy looking over Buckingham Palace—especially the stables, horses, harnesses and carriages. Lord Lonsdale suggested that the 101 riders meet him at Hyde Park at 10:00 a.m. the next day. He specified that they were to arrive individually, not as a group, and that they were to come on horseback and dress in their full Wild West costumes.

The following morning, the Wild West met London's sedate Rotten Row. Cowboys and cowgirls decked out in Stetsons, bright shirts and scarves, fringed jackets and beaded gloves slowly gathered, calling to each other and waving to the onlookers who gaped at them. Police called to the riders to stop the fancy-dress disturbance. Led by Guy, the riders were all innocence, assuring the police that they were interested only in going for a quiet morning ride. Slowly, but with perfect timing, the 101 riders closed in on Prince's Gate and created an immediate and glorious traffic jam. In the midst of it all, at exactly ten o'clock, Lord Lonsdale arrived. One of the most popular men in London at the time, he was greeted with roars of approval by the crowd and soon had everyone soothed. With Guy and the other riders in tow, he rode easily onto the grounds of Buckingham Palace.

Guy's skills as a promoter were often put to the test, and he used any means to attract audiences. In London, the Indian portion of the show wasn't holding the crowd's attention for some reason. The newspapers ignored it, despite Guy's best efforts. Something had to be done.

Guy complained to the press that the aboriginal peoples in the show were unhappy because they were sleeping indoors instead of in tipis in the great open spaces they were used to. He interested medical health officers in their sad plight, and health authorities instructed the hotel to pitch tents on the roof for the benefit of the First Peoples. The newspapers featured the story in sensational style. Show attendance picked up, and Guy was happy. The aboriginal performers, however, didn't like it a bit. All of them had come from modern houses in North American cities, and they felt uncomfortable

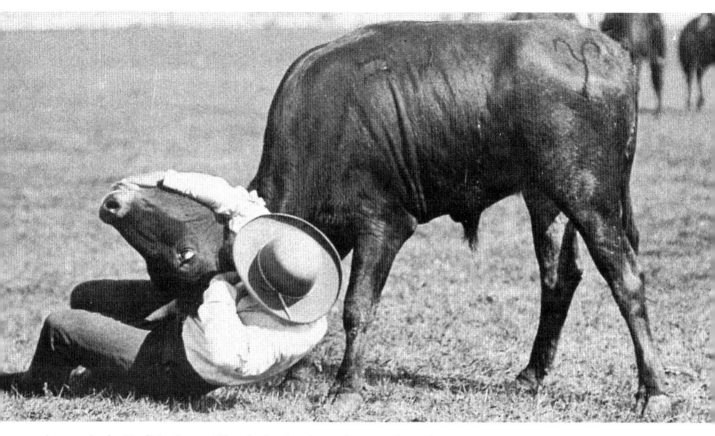

in tents in the English climate. They had to be given a bonus to keep them from stampeding back to the bedrooms.

Bill Pickett's bulldogging was routed by English humane societies, who had Pickett arrested for cruelty to animals. He was fined twenty-five dollars, and the incident received widespread newspaper coverage. Zack Miller and Guy saw the chance for cheap advertising and kept the act in the show, making a deal with British authorities that Pickett would be fined each week.

Despite the outcry, Pickett's bulldogging was popular in England and garnered him quite a following. At one point during the British tour, he was challenged to bulldog a wild Scottish Highland steer. It proved to be a simple

Jim Massey energetically attempts to bulldog a steer at the Winnipeg Stampede.

task for Pickett, and he received a warm ovation from the entire house.

Cowgirls received enthusiastic attention from British audiences as well, as Ellsworth Collings noted in his 1937 book on the 101 Ranch. "The most impressive of the cowgirls is Miss Florence LaDue, of Bliss, Oklahoma. 'Say,' she said to a representative of The Daily Citizen, 'I won my title at The Stampede, Calgary, Canada in 1912, and kept it the following year in Winnipeg. This is the belt I won,' she added as she proudly showed an engraved gold belt which encircled her waist.

"Florence is distinctly accomplished in prairie pastimes. She can 'rope' (lasso) a running horse, steer, or even a man with the best cowboy going, and she can make the lariat do all sorts of twists, loops, and turns, and she can shoot 'some.'"

Zack Miller was thinking of touring the continent with the 101 Ranch show when news of war put England on an emergency footing. The horses and vehicles of show were commandeered, and only through some fast talking were the Millers able to prevent their best horses from being pressed into military service. The troupe was forced to return to the United States.

The Miller Brothers had experienced losses in Britain, but they continued to put on shows across the U.S. during the 1915–16 season. They added Jess Willard, the world-champion prize fighter known as the Great White Hope, to help attract crowds in 1915, and one section of the show, Guy and Florence among them, branched off to perform in San Francisco.

During the show's California stay, Guy was contacted by the San Francisco World's Fair directors, who were considering putting on a world-championship cowboy contest. They suggested that Guy might like to run it. It was an interesting and challenging proposal, backed by a certified cheque for $175,000 to cover preliminary expenses. But Guy turned it down. San Francisco, he pointed out, wasn't cow country. The city was too far removed from the large population that would be needed to support the show. Everything would have to be hauled in, including audiences, and with the war on, transportation might be a problem.

During the winter of 1914–15, Guy and Florence returned with the show to the 101 Ranch, where several early western films were being shot. Film actors such as Buck Jones, Mabel Normand, Neal Hart, and Hoot and Helen Gibson got their start at the ranch, and Guy had a chance to study movie-making up close.

In 1916, an elderly Buffalo Bill Cody, now unable to mount his famous white stallion, joined the 101 show and delighted fans by shattering glass balls with his sharpshooting.

It was around this time that Guy began writing a cowboy events column for *Billboard*, America's top entertainment magazine, under the name "Rowdy Waddy" (an Australian term for cowboy). The growth of Wild West shows and rodeos demanded regular coverage, and Guy was only too pleased to contribute. He saw it as part of his personal commitment to "keeping the memory of the oldtimers green" and an opportunity to tell the true and changing story of the cowboy. He wrote about real cowboys—and like Chip of the Flying U, he had little patience for those who promoted or talked about the West without ever experiencing it. His columns covered performers such as Will Rogers, cowboys working in motion pictures like Tom Mix, and the trials and triumphs of cowboys and cowgirls who were making their names in frontier days and stampede contests. At the same time, as Mary Lou Lecompte notes in *Cowgirls of the Rodeo*, *Billboard* also began carrying a cowgirl column called "Wimmin's Writes" by Whistling Annie, who may have been Florence LaDue.

In his column, Guy acted as a watchdog on rodeo organizers. Rodeo was popular and widespread, but it wasn't governed by a formal organization until 1936. Some disreputable entrepreneurs saw the opportunity to take advantage of the growing sport. These producers, known as "bloomers," entered small communities and scheduled rodeos. They advertised heavily, charged high admissions and appeared legitimate until the entry fees and gate receipts were in. Then they skipped town, leaving contestants broke and bitter. Guy was concerned about such fraud and, over the years, provided a bulletin board of news about western life and the latest rodeo developments.

Although he was branching out a bit, Guy was as interested as ever in producing shows, and he was always on the lookout for new and challenging opportunities. One would come his way before too long.

Trick rider Emily McLeod performs before crowds at the New York Stampede, 1916.

The Big Apple and a Victory Stampede

I N 1916, GUY WEADICK undertook to put on his largest and most ambitious stampede yet. At the request of Broadway actor and comedian Fred Stone, Guy and Florence cancelled their vaudeville tour and went to New York, where Guy took on the job of organizing a stampede scheduled to take place at Sheepshead Bay Speedway, Long Island, from August 5 to 12. The prize money was an imposing $50,000, the largest purse ever offered.

The stampede was the first event of its kind in New York. Audiences had responded enthusiastically to Buffalo Bill's Wild West and the performances by the 101 Ranch Wild West show at Madison Square Gardens, but those had been designed as entertainment. This one would be a full-fledged cowboy competition. The sponsor for the eight-day event was the Speedway Western Exhibition Company.

New York was a formidable challenge for Guy, and he hit the town with everything he had. He stormed the papers with stories and advertising and called on every theatre operator, stage hand, performer and community leader he could think of to promote the event.

Ad Day and Charlie Irwin brought in the stock for the New York Stampede. Irwin's string of fast buckers were sent by special train direct from Cheyenne's Frontier Days, which had closed the previous week. Johnny Mullens, the stockman, arena director and top horseman who had worked the 1912 Calgary Stampede, was on hand with his experience. Trains from Fort Worth and Cheyenne brought in the top contest hands in the business, and baggage cars were full of the best horses. The experienced announcer Foghorn Clancy was hired for the event.

The contestants enjoyed their trip to New York and eagerly took in all the sights. A night or two before the opening of the stampede, they were invited to a special party at Coney Island's Luna Park, then America's greatest playground. As Foghorn Clancy would later recall in his book *My Fifty Years in Rodeo*, "All the rides at Luna Park were free to the cowboys and cowgirls and there were plenty of trick rides none of us had ever seen before. We were having a great time when our party was crashed by four hoodlums who had dug up cowboy hats somewhere and decided to get in on the free rides. They went to board one, but the attendant looked them over and decided that hats or no hats they didn't look like cowboys and said, 'No.' The characters started a roughhouse with the attendant, but the nearest cowboys pitched in and the hoodlums got their ride—one in an ambulance and three in the patrol wagon."

The stampede opened on the afternoon of August 5 to a crowd of 15,000. The arena and grandstand at Sheepshead Bay Speedway were enormous, and the audience must have looked lost in such a setting. They made up for it in enthusiasm and wild cheering.

The stampede events were full of raw challenge and excitement. Bucking horse competitions, a cowgirls' relay race, bulldogging, steer roping and bareback riding were mixed in with novelty events such as a cowboys' nightshirt race, a stagecoach race, trick riding, Indian races, a pony express race and a wild horse race. Fancy and trick roping and riding completed the program.

Floyd Irwin prepares for a daring turn in the trick riding competition at the New York Stampede.

The top cowgirls in the country were there to compete for prizes and world titles, and they gave audiences plenty to watch. The week's events began with a sensational ride by Dot Vernon. The black bucking horse she had drawn was let loose and began to plunge and rear, see-sawing. The crowd gasped: this was no ordinary form of entertainment. Dot hung on and earned the crowd's applause. Moments later, in the same event, the popular "Prairie Lillie" Allen went into what looked like a fatal accident. Her plunging horse went down on his forelegs, throwing her over his head and then rolling completely. Several women in the audience fainted, but Lillie quickly picked herself up and waved reassuringly to the crowd.

Chuckwagons appeared as part of the novelty events. Guy had arranged for a race that included making camp and lighting a fire between two chuckwagon outfits. He intended it as a tribute to traditional roundup practices, but he couldn't help noticing the interest it stirred.

On the second day, the crowd enjoyed more spectacular performances, not all of them in the rodeo arena. During his bulldogging performance, Bill Pickett threw his steer in twenty-six seconds, which caused a commotion down in the bullpens. Charlie Irwin got into a fist fight with another cowboy, Ed Lindsey, over whether Pickett had "hooliganed" the animal. (Hooliganing describes the practice in which the rider jumps on the steer's horns and pulls him down rather than twisting the animal by the neck.) The two were in a scrimmage when Charlie's son Floyd pitched into his father's assailant, and soon there was a lively mix-up going on among the cowboys.

August 10 was Movie Actors' Day, and Art Accord and Hoot Gibson took to the dust to prove that their rodeo skill was more than screen deep. Will Rogers and former U.S. president Theodore Roosevelt were also on hand to cheer on the competitors.

Rogers was in New York performing his fancy-roping and fancy-talking act with Ziegfeld's Midnight Frolic. He invited forty or so of his old rodeo companions to drop by, and the night they did, he cut his own act short to act as master of ceremonies for an impromptu rodeo evening. Guy was among those who joined Will on stage and tossed some fancy rope. Champion Australian cow whip man Vern Tantlinger caught his whip on a high wire inside the theatre and was unable to pull it down. "Get Shorty," the cowboys called, and "Texas Shorty" Hartley, who stood 6 feet, 11 3/4 inches tall in his stocking feet, got the whip free without stretching.

New Yorkers liked the stampede, and they had a chance to prove their loyalty on the final day. In one of the last events, Dick Hornbuckle of Douglas, Wyoming, was thrown under the legs of his bucking horse and stepped on by the animal. The cowboy's right leg was broken below the knee. The fall eliminated his chances of winning any prize money and meant he would be laid up in New York for several weeks. So it was decided to take up a collection for him. Cowgirls in costume swarmed into the grandstand as Foghorn Clancy called for donations from the spectators. The sombreros full of money weighed in at $834.30. The crowd greeted the announcement with a cheer.

The news wasn't so cheerful for the rest of the contestants, however. Despite strong promotion all week and good coverage in the papers, attendance had been slow. It may have just been bad timing. A heat wave with temperatures in the eighties and humidity readings in the nineties stunned the city and caused several deaths. Banner headlines proclaimed a dangerous outbreak of infantile paralysis, and the city was hit with a major transportation strike. Despite a promise from Guy that all prize money would be paid out on the morning of August 13, many winners went away empty-handed. Guy did everything he could to get the program extended for another week to try to recoup the losses, but despite negotiations with the director and officers of the Speedway Corporation, the stampede ended in the red.

The New York Stampede was Guy's first and only flop. It was the only rodeo he ever produced that did not pay off as advertised. The winners received only a quarter of the advertised purse money, earning Guy the lingering nickname of "26% Weadick." The sponsoring directors later informed federal authorities that they had lost $42,000.

Most of the contestants had paid their own expenses to New York and their own entry fees with no guarantees. Many had spent all their money on sightseeing. Heavy winners were surrounded by friends needing money to cover railway fares home or to the next competition. Most of them got it. Aboriginal participants fared better—they had travelled to the stampede at government expense and were guaranteed passage home.

Over the next few years, Guy and Florence continued to follow the Wild West and vaudeville circuits with their act. In April 1917, when the United States entered the war, they put together a show that included bucking horse riders and ropers, and they began to tour the army camps, entertaining the troops as well as staging exhibitions in support of bond-selling drives. They didn't know yet that the end of the war would take them back to Calgary and the reviving of Guy's dream.

In the summer of 1919, the Calgary Exhibition went all out to celebrate the peace in Europe. The famous American band of John Philip Sousa roused jubilant hearts with evening concerts, while overhead pilots "Wop" May and Freddy McCall took turns buzzing the grandstand, showing off the daring manoeuvres that had enabled them to survive dog fights over the Western Front. Horse races vied with automobile races to attract the most attention, and the new concrete grandstand and cattle pavilion bustled with visitors.

In the middle of the exhibition festivities came the announcement in Calgary newspapers that Guy Weadick was back in town. In full-page advertising, he announced that a great Calgary Victory Stampede would be held from August 25 to 30 at the Exhibition Grounds.

The idea of holding a Victory Stampede had not originated with Guy, although he was delighted to take it on. E. L. Richardson was the force behind it, seeing 1919 as the perfect year for a return engagement. Richardson contacted George Lane, who took on the task of persuading the other three original sponsors. Guy and Florence were performing in Spokane when Lane tracked Guy down to see if he would take on the job of organizing the celebration. He agreed, for a fee, to restage the event if the Big Four would again guarantee its solvency.

The Victory Stampede guaranteed $25,000 in purses for bucking horse riders, steer ropers and bulldoggers. Also featured would be stand-up chariot-type races, cowgirls' saddlebronc riding and relay races, and the usual trick roping and riding acts. Top performers from across the country began to send in their entry fees. As the show dates approached, Guy put on a spectacular

The famous Ed Borein drawing of a twisting bronc, "I-See-U," quickly became a Stampede icon.

The bucking horse competition was one of the most popular main events. Here Thunder takes Lloyd Meyers for a high ride.

advertising and publicity drive that culminated in a special twelve-page *Calgary Herald* Victory Stampede supplement.

In the years since the 1912 stampede, Guy had learned a thing or two about running a smooth operation. This time around, rigidly constructed saddling chutes were provided to get the broncs saddled quickly and the events run off the same way. Events were divided into daily heats, with top contestants scheduled to compete for the championship on the final day.

The show drew 57,456 spectators, far short of expected attendance. Uncertainty over crop prospects may have been one reason. The high cost of living in postwar inflation was frightening many, and the Victory Stampede, like its 1912 predecessor, charged a dollar admission and an additional fifty cents for a grandstand seat.

But like the earlier Calgary Stampede, this one was a heartfelt tribute to the cowboy. Montana cowboy writer Teddy Blue Abbott had worked the big cattle drives from Texas and found much at the stampede that reminded him of the old days:

> If I had not seen anything but Charlie Russell's pictures I would have been well paid for the trip. One picture owned by George Lane is a horse bucking through camp. He upset the coffee pot…Dutch oven, frying pan and scattered the fire, and the cook is standing by the mess wagon with a butcher knife in his hand. Say, that picture is so true I could hear that cook swear. I knew just what he was saying, and them old roundup cooks could sure say things. It made the tears come in my eyes to think that once I was a part of that life in those good old days…There was about 1,000 Blackfeet Indians there in all their bright colors and fancy fixings. I saw a lot of old Buffalo Indians there and when they saw the picture of Blackfeet Indians running buffalo, you could see those old men get in a bunch in front of it and they would straighten up and their eyes would shine like stars. They talked and made signs—it was great to watch them. Many of them had run buffalo and I guess they felt about like I did over the horse bucking through camp. It's sure better to be an old has-been than a never-was.

Like other events of its kind, the Victory Stampede was a chance for some serious storytelling to take place among men who spoke the same language.

Cowboy Fun

Guy Weadick's qualities as a showman were appreciated as much by stampede competitors as by the audience. In his 1986 *Calgary Herald* article "Past Glory," Dan'l La Rocque quotes Stan Fullerton, who was an eager young cowboy at the 1919 stampede: "There were these two fellas…they used to get pretty tough with each other around the corrals all the time. Now Guy Weadick knew this, and he decided that if they were going to squabble, we might just as well all of us get into the fun. So he talked them into doing their fighting in the barns, and there were tickets, but only for the Stampede people. One of those lads was big and tough, and the other was scientific. Good fighter too. The scientific fella won fair and square. That Guy Weadick. Never missed a chance to put on a show if he had any chance at all."

As Abbott described it in the *Havre Plaindealer*, "Once more the thunder roared and the lightning flashed and the beef herd run again…You could hear the calves bawl and smell the hair burn—gosh, it was great—stories of the old Texas trail and the range from the Guadeloupe in Texas to Fort McLeod in Canada went the rounds."

Guy Weadick had now staged four major stampedes, but no city was ready to commit to an annual event. Wild West shows were in decline. Buffalo Bill had died in 1917, and the public appetite for western fare seemed to be waning. Cowboy competitions were still popular at Cheyenne, Prescott and Pendleton, but there was no professional rodeo association or established circuit.

The city of Saskatoon approached Guy about putting on a stampede for them during a fair they were planning to entertain the Prince of Wales, but Weadick turned them down. The time was too short to put together an attraction of the calibre he was accustomed to presenting.

Once the Victory Stampede dust had settled, Guy and Florence took their roping act back to vaudeville for the winter. But the western Canadian foothills had taken hold of their hearts, and in the spring of 1920, after a dozen years of married life and constant travel, they finally decided to put down roots.

The Stampede Ranch in Eden Valley was home, haven and dude ranch centre for the Weadicks for twenty years.

The Stampede Ranch

IN THE SPRING OF 1920, direct from New York, Guy and Florence bought a working ranch on the Highwood River, about twenty miles by winding gravel road from the village of Longview, south of Calgary. They named it the Stampede Ranch, and from then on, although they continued to travel, the Stampede Ranch was home.

It was a magnificent location. From their front porch, the Weadicks could watch the sun set over the hills. The waters of the Highwood River and Flat Creek freshened the air, and across the valley they could see George Lane's historic Bar U Ranch and the border of the EP Ranch owned by the Prince of Wales.

8

It was perfect peace for Guy and Florence, and a beautiful setting for the western life they loved so well. Here they raised cattle and horses and kept chickens and assorted dogs and cats. Here they could return with a contented sigh every spring after a long winter of daily performances and staying in cheap hotels. Here they could be themselves.

From the first, Guy and Florence planned to run the Stampede Ranch as a dude ranch. The idea of dude ranching appealed to their outgoing natures; it would allow them to welcome visitors from around the world and to bring in some welcome extra money.

Dude ranching still provoked raised eyebrows in the Canadian foothills, although it was already well established in the western United States, where it had been introduced in the 1880s. Buffalo Bill Cody had helped to set the pace once again in 1902 when he had built the luxurious Irma Hotel in Cody, Wyoming. Named after his youngest daughter, this impressive modern establishment boasted a telephone in every room and assured guests that "everything is clean and first class." By the time Guy and Florence set up business, there was already a Dude Ranchers' Association in the United States.

Western American tourism had received a big boost in 1906 when a "See America First" conference at Salt Lake City proclaimed the wonders of homegrown scenery. During the first three decades of the century, seventeen new national parks were added, national forests were expanded, and strong emphasis was placed on outdoor family recreation. Automobiles made travel a lot easier, and the western landscape held out the promise of the cowboy, new experiences and a dose of frontier history.

In Canada, the building of safe, sturdy roads was seen as key to bringing some of the American traffic north. Calgary's first automobile club began in 1908, and after the First World War, auto clubs from Canada and Montana banded together to boost the "Sunshine Trail," which was to run from Mexico to Alaska. By the 1920s, a road system had been developed in the mountain parks, inviting travellers, particularly wealthy Europeans, Americans and central Canadians, to discover for themselves the wonders of the Rocky Mountains.

Guy understood the tenderfoot's interest in the West; it was the same passion that drew him every year to the foothills. But he and Florence also knew about marketing. Although they were running a dude ranch, they were careful not to mention the term in their advertising. Their promotional brochure was reassuring and inviting:

> The Stampede Ranch is a practical cattle ranch, enjoying real ranch life. Accommodations have been made for only 35 guests. It is not a resort.
>
> Ranch buildings devoted to guest accommodations include main ranch house, log cabins and cottages, while for those who desire them, there are large genuine Indian painted tepees. All beds, linen, etc., are comparable to those used in a first-class hotel. Rooms are furnished with both double and twin beds.
>
> The large log living room at the main ranch house (40 x 30) is where guests gather to spend the evening, after a day in the open. Large native stone fireplace, piano, victrola and radio. Hardwood floor makes it ideal for dancing.
>
> Tub and shower baths, hot and cold water at all hours. Electric lights, comfortable beds, and furniture. Long-distance telephone and telegraph service. First-class medical service and hospital close by.
>
> "Come where there are no snakes nor poisonous insects" Season: May 15-Oct. 1.

Guy promoted the ranch with his characteristic enthusiasm. He sent out flyers to everyone he knew and wrote articles on the ranch for local newspapers. He promised guests special roping and branding events, chuckwagon and trail rides, a choice of cabins or tipis to sleep in. He extolled the natural beauty of the eastern slopes of the Rocky Mountains and even made the coal oil seepages, a distinctive geological formation in the area, sound intriguing. The letterhead for the Stampede Ranch was as elaborate as any Wild West program. Photographs of mountain scenery, native people, bucking horses and cowboy life crowded the edges of the page, underscoring the motto, "A Real Place for Real Folks."

Not content with the natural wonders that surrounded the ranch, in the first year Guy offered winter visitors trips into the mountains with Husky pack dogs to "Virgin Valleys, which have never been explored by tourists." It

was, he allowed, "a form of sport, that as yet, has never before been introduced by guides and outfitters. Dog trains can be had for winter trips, but these trips are only suitable for people prepared to put in a certain amount of hardship and real roughing it."

The walls of the main lodge were covered with framed photographs of rodeo contestants, show people and English royalty. Four of the best rooms were named after the Big Four, and each was branded with one of the Big Four brands: A7, NL, Bar U and CY. Guy wrote to Lane, Burns, Cross and McLean, urging them to visit and asking for photos to hang in the rooms dedicated to them. By July, the main ranch house was up and ready. Visitors arrived by train at High River or Calgary, a three-hour drive away. Soon guests

The main room of the ranch house was the site of many parties for guests, friends and neighbours. It was decorated with memorabilia of the Weadicks' many travels and photos of their famous friends.

from New York and Los Angeles, including actors and western writers, began appearing on familiar riding trails around the foothills.

Guy and Florence were lucky in their neighbours. Joe and Josephine Bews and their children lived nearby on the Rocking P Ranch, and the Bar U joined the Stampede Ranch on the north side. In the 1920s, Frazier and Emma Hunt bought the Pocaterra place across the river and became close friends with Guy and Florence. Frazier Hunt was associate editor of *Cosmopolitan* magazine, which later donated prizes to the stampede. And, like many of the foothills ranchers, Guy was delighted to claim the Prince of Wales as a neighbour.

In 1919, the prince had visited the Bar U Ranch as a guest of George Lane, and two weeks later he arranged to purchase the Bedingfield Ranch, a magnificent spread where he planned to establish a private retreat and a working ranch for breeding stock. But although he owned the property for forty-three years, the prince (later King Edward VIII, then the Duke of Windsor) visited the ranch only three times.

Raymond Patterson, along with his wife, later bought the nearby Buffalo Head Ranch from George Pocaterra and began running a dude operation next to the Weadicks. In his book *Far Pastures* he recalled some of the antics in the valley:

> They were the best of neighbours and, wherever possible, we co-operated. Their guests would ride over to visit us, and many was the good party that we and our people had up at the Stampede Ranch. But best of all were those winter evenings when the dudes had gone and the Eden Valley was itself again…
>
> Above the fireplace in the long room at the Stampede Ranch there was an old buffalo skull set into the rough river-stone of the chimney. Red electric lights were set in its eyeless sockets and the thing grinned ghoulishly in the flickering light of the log fire. Undeterred by this horror—or possibly even stimulated by it—Guy would tell tales of the Dolly Sisters, or of the days when he and Florence were on the same bill in vaudeville as Rosa Ponzillo and her sister…
>
> He was a born mimic in voice, hands and bearing, and soon we had the pleasure of seeing him mincing about the long room in the character of the

Yours and Mine

The hospitality of the Stampede Ranch was proclaimed in a motto Guy had written and mounted on a wall:

"This is your home and my home, your shelter and my shelter, your refuge and my refuge, though I have built it with my own hands. It was built for you as well as for me. When I blazed the trail by which you found it, I had you in mind.

"Care for that which is your own while you are here, and when you leave, clean up a little, for your brother or my brother, your pal or mine may be here shortly after you are gone.

"This is a cool spot in the summer. It is shelter from the storms of winter. It is yours and it is mine!"

future Rosa Ponselle [sic] or her sister on their first full-stage set, ordering the re-arrangement of piano, chairs and other properties, and objecting, now, to being sandwiched in between the animal act and the monologist. He would then become the owner of the performing dogs, complaining that his terriers were as house-broke as any one else on the bill, and good enough so that nobody need be ashamed to follow them. Then the soft, southern voice of the monologist would come out of the wavering shadows of the long room, saying that he'd been happy once till the manager messed the bill up, and now he wished to God he was back in Georgia where there was peace. The monologist did not end there, but most of what he said was strictly libellous and best left alone.

Guy's abilities as a talker were legendary, and he had plenty of opportunities to hold forth out at the Stampede Ranch, as Bert Sheppard, a neighbour who often visited, recalls: "If Guy had the floor it was about impossible to get it away from him. I remember riding up to the Stampede Ranch, Freddie Nash and Guy were standing close together outside the house. It looked like they had been drinking. Nash was holding his horse ready to leave. Guy was talking very fast and had his thumb cocked. Every time Fred would open his mouth to say something, Guy would jab him in the stomach with his thumb and he never got it said, so climbed on his horse and rode away."

Mary Dover, the daughter of A. E. Cross, told another amusing story about Guy's talking skills.

> Guy loved having guests and Peter B. Kyne the western writer and Frazier Hunt used to come over. They were wonderful storytellers and used to tease each other and talk…
>
> There was one particular evening—I think Frazier Hunt was at the bottom of all this nonsense. They had a dinner, I know Daddy came over from the A7—probably 15 people, they couldn't accommodate more than that, it was a modest place.
>
> Peter Kyne and Guy used to always interrupt each other; they wouldn't stop talking. They were a bad pair to have in one room.
>
> I think it was Frazier who said, "Look we'll have a competition. We'll see who can talk longest." So after dinner, everybody made bets. Peter Kyne had a

A Royal Rancher

As Simon Evans recounts in his book *Prince Charming Goes West*, Guy liked his royal neighbour the Prince of Wales, and in September 1923 he rode over with some cowboys to present a special rodeo for the prince, who was hosting a picnic and stock show for members of the short-horn breeders association. Among the performers was Pete Vandermeer, the overall winner at the Calgary Stampede that year, to whom the prince presented an engraved silver cigarette case. As the prince warmly congratulated the cowboy, the practical Vandermeer pulled back and in some embarrassment said, "I'm sorry, Prince, but I don't smoke." The prince was at a loss, until Guy stepped in and settled the problem by whispering, "Tell Pete we'll get him a gold watch."

Guy, striking a characteristic pose, engages the Prince of Wales on a western topic during one of the Prince's few visits to his Alberta ranch.

Entertaining Dudes

One of Guy's favourite duties on the ranch
was to introduce visitors to western life.
The ranch could accommodate about
thirty guests, and dudes were provided
with ranch chaps, neckerchiefs and wide
hats before joining in on trail rides, chuckwagon meals, roping demonstrations and
other activities. Florence tended to the
administrative and financial details, while
Guy provided the running commentary to
amused guests. The Weadicks never made
a good living from the dudes, but running a
guest ranch suited their outgoing natures.

passion for somewhere in California so he started to talk, and about two hours later he ran out, literally.

Someone said, "That's all very well, but you know the Stampede is pretty good. It stacks up a little bit with California."

At which Guy jumped in and five or six hours later he was still at it. Finally they all got up and went to bed.

Being a practical sort, Florence ran the ranch with attention to details and comfort. While Guy was known everywhere as "Guy," she was always called "Mrs. Weadick." She looked after the financial end of things, oversaw the cooking and cleaning, and made sure that all the wranglers wore clean shirts and bright scarves. She ensured that guests always had the right-sized saddles and horses—as much for the horse's comfort as for the rider's. Nothing angered her more than a mistreated animal, but she could be a bit tough on her employees, as rancher Bert Sheppard later remembered.

One time they had some girls there, some college girls I guess and three chaperones, probably a dozen girls. They had a little old bald-headed Bar U cowboy there to take them out for rides.

These girls—old Gordon had to take them out, see that their cinches were tight and they didn't get into trouble and they'd be asking questions all the time—well, it was just one hell of a job. He had these people out all day and after supper he'd had about enough of it. After supper Mrs. Weadick turned to him and said, now you can take out the chaperones and Gordon said, what do you think I am for Christ's sake, Superman?

The Weadicks were a devoted couple. They admired each other tremendously, and even Florence's occasional "For God's sake, Guy, shut up!" was said with tolerance and humour. They were well matched, and they valued their marriage as the true partnership it was. But Guy's enthusiasms and gregarious nature frequently got him into romantic and other kinds of scrapes, and others watched with amusement as he extricated himself. An inlaid coffee table and silver candlesticks were among the evidence of Guy's attempts to placate his strong-minded wife. After one incident in which Guy had apparently escorted another woman in his car, Florence refused to set foot in that

Rough dirt roads played havoc with early ranch vehicles. Hands quickly became expert at changing tires along the way to pick up and deliver guests.

vehicle again. For months neighbours watched in amazement at the manner in which the Weadicks went to town: Guy drove ahead in one car, opening each of the twenty-two gates along the gravel road, while Florence followed in a second vehicle, closing the gates behind her.

Lenore McLean, née Bews, who grew up on the Rocking P Ranch adjoining the Weadick ranch, later recalled how modern the Stampede Ranch seemed. "They had a little Delco generator and had electric lights they ran off batteries. And they had an indoor toilet and running water inside! They built shower stalls in a row by the cabins for the guests and they would heat up the water on a wood stove. They had rigged up a dumb waiter/cooler. It was a deep wide hole in the ground and they'd lower a box with shelves on it into the hole where it was cool. You could crank it up and there would be shelves of eggs and milk and vegetables."

In the fall of 1920, Guy and Florence returned to the winter vaudeville circuit. When the Weadicks got back to the ranch in the following spring, they were contacted by Ernie Richardson, who hired them to put on their trick roping act as an intermission feature at the Calgary Spring Horse Show.

Guy was happy to see his name was not forgotten by the Calgary crowd. Ever the promoter, he wanted to make sure the whole district knew what he could offer, especially on his own spread. On August 19, 1922, he organized a special stampede on the Stampede Ranch, inviting everyone who was anyone for miles around. Invitations flooded out to all the leading businesses and social organizations in the area, and special service trucks and guide cars were scheduled to leave from the Palliser Hotel in Calgary at nine o'clock on the morning of the nineteenth. The High River Motor Co. agreed to supply vehicles as well as to provide a full outfit of repair parts and tires to car drivers who had difficulty with the long gravel road up to the ranch.

Among the events featured were bronc riding, wild steer riding, wild cow milking and a half-mile democrat free-for-all race. Prizes, many donated by Calgary and High River businesses, were presented to all winners as well as to the oldest pioneer attending and the Ford coming the longest distance. A big dance featuring Jack Bullough's orchestra from Calgary finished off the day's entertainment, and of course cabins and tipis were available for overnight accommodation.

For the next twenty years, the ranch would be home, entertainment centre, movie location and haven for Guy and Florence.

On the New York docks, while roping in some sailors, Guy Weadick also managed to rope in some international news attention for the Calgary Stampede.

The Stampede Takes Off

ERNIE RICHARDSON CAME calling at the Stampede Ranch in the late fall of 1922 with a proposal. Attendance at the Calgary Exhibition had been declining, and the directors were worried. They wondered if Guy could develop his western show into a full dress rodeo that could be combined with the Exhibition to bring back the crowds.

Guy was agreeable, but he drove a strong bargain. He wanted $5,000 for a six-month contract beginning in April. And he wanted to be free to continue his vaudeville and ranch work in the winter. In a surprising gamble for the Exhibition Board and the city, the directors agreed. Guy would be making as much for a half a year's work as Richardson received for full-time employment. He would be earning as much as the mayor of Calgary.

As soon as the handshakes were over, Guy swung into action. He was under considerable pressure to make the stampede the best ever and to recover enough receipts to put the books in the black. He may have had another motive for doing well: he hadn't yet achieved his dream of an annual cowboy contest, and he wanted Calgary to be the site for it. The 1923 event rolled several attractions into one program and was billed as the Calgary Exhibition, Stampede and Buffalo Barbecue.

The 1923 stampede couldn't offer the same cash prizes as the 1912 and 1919 events, so Guy began canvassing for other kinds of prizes that would draw competitors and audiences alike. The Prince of Wales agreed to donate a trophy to the saddle bronc champion; Canadian actress Mary Pickford and her husband, Douglas Fairbanks, would award the trophies for the Roman standing race and the relay race; local businesses such as the Great West Saddlery and Riley and McCormick contributed trophy saddles. Buffalo heads, Navajo blankets, cases of mounted birds and a dozen other items were rounded up. The show was to kick off once again with an enormous parade on Monday morning and end on Saturday night with a barbecue of buffalo meat.

To promote the stampede, Guy chose an image by the noted western artist Ed Borein of a wildly twisting bronc. The drawing, entitled "I-See-U," became one of the best-known images of the stampede.

Exciting new acts were offered at the 1923 stampede: a wild horse race, a wild cow milking contest, an Indian slow race in which the last horse to wander across the finish line won—and a spectacular fireworks display. But the act that took the infield by storm was event number 10, the cowboy's chuckwagon race.

Some of the ranchers who were invited to participate in the chuckwagon race were reluctant at first. It meant taking up the time of busy ranch hands and contributing a useful wagon to some kind of damn fool race that would almost certainly destroy all the equipment and probably a few bones as well.

Eventually six wagons entered the Romping Rangeland Rumpus and were divided into two heats of three outfits each. The rules were clear. Each wagon was to cut a figure 8 around a barrel, head through the backstretch onto the track, run around the track and return to the campground. They then had to

CALGARY STAMPEDE
16

"unhook team from wagon. Stretch fly. No less than 2 stakes, and make fire. First smoke decides winner."

Things didn't work out exactly as planned. As Doug Nelson describes in his book *From Hot Cakes to High Stakes*, Clem Gardner and his V Quarter Circle rig were the first to send up camp smoke in the first race but were disqualified because the team was facing the wrong way. The Mosquito Creek wagon outriders whipped their team and caused the wagon to spill, prompting a new rule that outriders couldn't interfere with their wagon driver once a race had started. In Nelson's book, Art Hudson, a member of the Mosquito Creek outfit, remembered, "There was something wrong with every race we

The chuckwagon races started off the mark in 1923 and have led the Stampede excitement ever since.

ran. There were meetings going on every night in every barn." George Lane and A. E. Cross helped drivers and organizers to work out rules for the new sport. After five dusty, dangerous days, the Mosquito Creek outfit, driven by Dan Riley of High River, was declared the winner of the first Rangeland Derby and a new western tradition was born.

Another surprising success of the stampede was a huge Cowboys and Old Timers dance held on the Friday night in the Palliser Hotel ballroom. Tickets sold out almost immediately, four more bands were hired, and the dancing spilled out onto the street. Four thousand people bowed and sashayed and swirled around the roped-off street from 10:00 p.m. until two in the morning.

The Buffalo Barbecue, which closed the week-long program, was also a big hit. The buffalo, cooked at Pat Burns's packing plant, was made into 11,000 sandwiches for free distribution on the grounds. It was an enormous volunteer effort, with everyone from the mayor to the cowboys pitching in.

Throughout stampede week, Guy Weadick was everywhere—waving to 30,000 spectators as he led the kick-off parade with Mayor George Webster, riding his horse up to the grandstand to sweep his hat with a flourish to spe-

Street dances contributed to Stampede celebrations for several years. Mary Dover recalled, "It was a wonderful thing. You came to watch, only to find yourself, suddenly, dancing."

cial guests, slapping the backs of cowboys near the chutes, urging business-men to "dress western" and closing the day at the Palliser Hotel exchanging stories. A record 137,825 people were attracted through the gates, and they filled the grandstand to capacity most days.

Guy had accomplished what he had set out to do—establish the stampede as an exciting, profitable event that would be talked about across North America. The Exhibition Board was pleased too—especially at the surplus of over $22,000.

Guy's arrangement with the Exhibition Board ended when the stampede closed down in July. He and Florence left to resume their vaudeville careers, and the board had until December 1 to let him know if they wanted to extend his contract. They did. The 1924 stampede set the pace for the next decade by attracting 167,000 visitors to the six-day show. One of the highlights was an impressive display of the teamster's profession in the person of Slim Moorehouse, who drove a thirty-two-horse team hauling ten loaded grain wagons through the streets of Calgary.

Watching closely from the grandstand seats at the 1924 stampede was an enterprising Calgary horseman named Pete Welsh. Welsh and his family owned a stable of high-jumping horses, including the famous Barra Lad, the animal they hoped would win the world title. Welsh was impressed with the excitement of the crowd as they cheered for contestants in the bucking horse, wild cow milking and bull riding competitions. He did some quick calcula-tions, balancing the cost of shipping livestock and contestants to other cities against the sure-fire profits a travelling exhibition would bring. He signed up Fred Kennedy, a reporter for the *Albertan*, as his publicity man and struck a deal with "Strawberry Red" Wall, a cowboy from Washington, to launch Calgary's first competitive rodeo outfit. Welsh began buying up top bucking stock, and after incorporating as the Alberta Stampede Company Limited, went off to promote his enterprise in Winnipeg, New Westminster, B.C., Ottawa, Toronto and Detroit.

Guy Weadick was on the vaudeville circuit when he heard of Welsh's stam-pede and read articles about it in the *Albertan*. He was outraged. "It makes me dam mad," he wrote to E. L. Richardson, "to get out and hustle my head off in an endeavour to interest thousands of people from distances to come to Calgary to see this show, and then to have a Calgary paper, one that looks for and receives quite a compensation for advertising from us, besides us putting on a show that means much to the paper's own town, come out and try and cop everything we do."

Guy instructed Richardson to persuade the publisher of the *Albertan* to shut off Welsh's publicity notices and to take the matter to Alberta Premier John Brownlee. Richardson also headed a delegation to Edmonton to persuade the premier to forbid the use of the world "Stampede" for any more corporate registrations.

The matter came to a head when Guy received a letter from K. A. Cook, assistant general agent of Canadian Pacific Lines, inquiring about Guy's needs for transportation arrangements for the stampede scheduled to appear in Detroit in October 1925. Welsh's stampede had apparently been booked for the Olympia Theater there, and the agent, who knew Guy slightly, believed him to be in charge. Guy immediately wrote the manager of the Olympia:

> I have just been informed that your Olympia will open in October with a cowboy contest staged for you by the Calgary Stampede organization.
>
> For your information, beg to state that *The Stampede* was originated by me at Calgary in 1912, first cowboy contest and frontier celebration to ever use that title. All our literature, photos, etc. is fully protected by copyright both in the U.S. and Canada and we will prosecute all infringements.
>
> There was an outfit last year with a sort of a travelling wild west show that went to Winnipeg, Montreal and Toronto, and lost considerable money for the sponsors so I am informed, who called themselves the Alberta Stampede Co., headed by a fellow named Welsh…He never had any connection with the Calgary Stampede in any shape or form.

Welsh responded by launching a suit against Guy Weadick and the Calgary Industrial Exhibition Company for $100,000 in damages. The suit might have been resolved over a friendly conversation and a drink in the snake pit at the Palliser. Guy could have pointed out to Welsh that the sense of camaraderie, pride in western heritage, ties with the ranching community and

Slim Moorhouse demonstrates his teamster skill by driving a thirty-two-horse team through Calgary, hauling ten loaded grain wagons.

volunteerism so necessary to presenting the show was a Calgary characteristic. It couldn't just be shipped to Winnipeg, New York or San Francisco. It was a lesson Welsh finally learned for himself in 1927, when the sheriff closed down his show and the suit was dropped. As a result of Richardson's representations to Premier Brownlee, the word "Stampede" was granted copyright protection. No company incorporated in Alberta was allowed to use it without the Exhibition Company's consent.

The 1920s were good years for Guy and Florence and for the Calgary Stampede. Each new stampede outdid the previous ones in attracting new

acts and new audiences. Each year, crowds kept coming back for more and going away satisfied. Lavishly illustrated brochures announced "An International Event of Distinction held in its Natural Environment, Devoid of Sham, Rehearsal, Exaggeration or Affectation." The Calgary Exhibition and Stampede, everyone declared, was the real thing. Gate receipts were healthy and the books were well in the black. Guy was given a bonus of $1,000 over his $5,000 yearly salary in 1927 and 1929.

He earned every cent of it. Despite having only a six-month contract each year, Guy never stopped working for the stampede. Every stop on the vaudeville circuit was another opportunity to pound the word of the Calgary Stampede into the ears of cattlemen and stage hands, mayors and congressmen, theatre impresarios and Rotary club members, actors and writers, train conductors and waiters. Every community group luncheon, every nodding head, was followed up with a phone call, a letter, an invitation. Back in Calgary, Ernie Richardson often found himself scrambling to respond to requests from people he had never heard of and to answer Guy's weekly, sometimes daily, conversations by letter.

Theirs was a colourful and voluminous correspondence. Although technically Guy's boss, Richardson recognized him as a colleague who shared his commitment to the stampede and scrupulously informed Guy about every activity. They discussed everything, from where to get the best Brahma bull stock to a complaint from a Calgary businessmen that the stampede shouldn't promote a prize from Levi Strauss because it unfairly advanced American jeans over Canadian products. Together the two handled all the details for the hundreds of trophies and prizes that Guy secured over the years.

Richardson often received word of Guy's activities through press clippings from across the country and even around the world. "We are continually getting more publicity clippings," he wrote to Weadick. "A week or so ago, Miss Harrison of the London Daily Express sent me a copy of the new English magazine Britannia, with a splendid two page article on the Stampede…A day or so ago, I got a menu from the New Washington Hotel, Seattle, on which the back page was devoted to an article 'Do You Know Calgary?'…and a paragraph on the Calgary Exhibition and Stampede."

The Silver Screen

Guy was quick to latch on to any scheme that would promote both the stampede and his beloved western foothills. At the time he and Florence opened the Stampede Ranch, western movies were hitting their full stride on the silver screen. Guy quickly lassoed his old Wild West pals Hoot Gibson and Neal Hart to start making movies in Alberta and to include segments of the stampede in the action. The most successful of these was the 1925 Universal Studios film *The Calgary Stampede*, which starred Hoot Gibson and featured, in a very small part, Guy himself. A mixture of melodramatic derring-do and exciting footage from the chariot and chuckwagon races of the real stampede, the film became a box-office hit across North America.

While in New York in 1926 on vaudeville business, Guy read in the paper that the *Empress of Scotland*, the big Canadian Pacific ship, was setting sail on her second around-the-world cruise. Donning his big Stetson, he headed down to the docks. He casually began roping up sailors who enjoyed the fun and asked to be taught rope tricks. It wasn't long before a crowd had gathered, and reporters from *Pathe News Weekly* and the International News Service began snapping photographs and asking questions about the tall, friendly cowboy. Within days, newspapers around the world were carrying headlines about the Calgary Stampede.

Each year, Guy remembered his promise to keep the old-timers' memories green. In 1925, the stampede celebrated the fiftieth anniversary of the arrival of the North-West Mounted Police at the future site of Calgary. The RCMP attended in a blaze of scarlet, bringing their famous Musical Ride. Surviving members of the great Mounted Police trek of 1874–75 were sought out and given positions of honour. The special guest that year was the field marshall of the British Forces in the First World War, Lord Douglas Haig and his wife, Lady Haig. After being made a chief of the Sarcees, Lord Haig breakfasted on chuckwagon fare and mingled enthusiastically with the Indians, cowboys, cowgirls and tourists who combined to make the downtown celebrations the most spectacular in Calgary history.

The strain of entertaining on such a lavish and exuberant scale every year began to take its toll, however. Downtown businesspeople, although they enjoyed a brisk trade, began to complain of the demands that were put upon them to create a frontier atmosphere. The roughhousing of lively cowboys and visitors raised some irritation, particularly among restaurant owners who were putting in long days and nights to feed and entertain customers. Guy tackled the problem head on. He encouraged the merchants to organize their own committee to run the downtown show, and a more orderly western environment developed.

Just after the 1925 stampede, Guy was awarded a gold watch by members of the Rotary, Kiwanis and Gyro clubs, the Western Stock Growers Association, the Hotel Association and the mayor of Calgary as a tribute for his efforts.

Guy and Florence were on the road in January 1926 when Guy was approached by Wild West show pioneer Pawnee Bill to help out with the publicity for an old-timers' celebration in Oklahoma in April. Guy wrote E. L. asking him what he thought. Richardson was supportive and political in his response: depending on the timing, the Exhibition Directors saw no conflict with the arrangement. "I think it would be just as well if the Calgary people were not aware of your running another Stampede," Richardson cautioned. "They can be allowed to think that you are on your vaudeville work as usual."

But in the end, Guy refused the Oklahoma engagement and hurried back to Calgary. Pete Welsh was still causing concern, and Guy wanted a big draw for the 1926 stampede. He arranged for a shipment of fast, wild Brahma steers to arrive secretly. He had seen them at a rodeo in Madison Square Gardens and, with their exotic humps and wild bucking, he knew the sensation they would cause in Calgary. He was also uneasy about the increasing role being played by Jack Dillon in stampede arrangements. Dillon was an experienced and knowledgeable arena man who had served as a judge for competitions at the stampede and Exhibition for years. Dillon too was anxious about the inroads Welsh was making on good bucking stock, and he was eager to secure as many good horses as he could for the stampede. Guy saw a possible threat to his own position.

Guy wanted it both ways. In October 1925, he finally received a letter from the Exhibition Board offering him a permanent half-yearly position as stampede manager. The contract would be renewed on an annual basis, with either party bound to request any changes to the arrangement by December 1. Weadick was pleased with the contract, but he asked that an addition be made to indicate that he would not undertake similar events only in western Canada. Although he resented Welsh's intrusion into the stampede business, he wanted to leave the door open for himself.

The 1928 stampede broke all records: attendance reached almost 200,000; profits were over $35,000; there were more cash prizes, more exhibits, and better horse races and rodeo events than ever before. Cameramen came from New York and Los Angeles to make newsreels to show on the movie screens of the world.

His Destiny

In 1928, Guy took the reins himself, producing and acting in a full-length movie called *His Destiny* or, for the American market, *North of 49*. Shot on location at the Stampede Ranch, the A7 Ranch and the grounds of the Calgary Stampede, it starred Neal Hart, Barbara Kent and members of the Calgary Elks Lodge. Pat Burns, A. E. Cross and John McFarland were persuaded to finance the film and, in the end, were able to recover their investment. It enjoyed a grand opening at the Palace Theatre in Calgary and was, as Guy noted, "not the worst movie ever made."

Western writer Walt Coburn attended the 1928 stampede at Guy's invitation, and he later described the behind-the-scenes action in an article in *West* magazine. Coburn and his wife, Pat, were given a suite of rooms at the Palliser, and an official stampede car was made available to them. Guy introduced the writer to cattlemen, old-time cowhands and rodeo contestants. Most impressive of all to the writer were liquor stores filled with shelves of genuine Scotch and Canadian rye whisky. The United States was still dry, but Calgary offered a spirited welcome to American visitors.

The Palliser acted as unofficial stampede headquarters. Cowboy contestants such as Breezy Cox, Earl Thode, Ike Rude, Paddy Ryan, Pinky Gist the rodeo clown, Pete and Harry Knight, and Jack Van Ryder, the cowboy artist from Arizona, shared rooms with one another. Ken Riley, son of Senator Dan Riley from High River, was there with Walt Deegan, who worked on Dan Riley's ranch. Neal Hart, the western movie star, was there too, having just completed a film shot in Banff and on Guy and Florence's ranch.

The overflowing rooms were also the scene of some Wild West action. Coburn recounted one story concerning high-stakes gambler and fancy dresser Roy Adams, a contestant from Arizona.

I was in Roy's room having a drink when I happened to mention that I'd had to leave my Colt .45 six-shooter with the customs officers at the port of entry into the United States, to be picked up on my return. Roy told me that he had managed to bring a little .32 automatic pistol across the line, and before I was aware of what he was doing he tilted the little belly gun toward the ceiling and fired a shot, explaining he knew the rooms above were sample rooms for travelling salesmen.

When we left the room and boarded the elevator there were two salesmen with their sample cases complaining that a civilized gentleman wasn't safe with these wild, drunken cowboys raising hell, hollering and shooting. Roy nudged me and dropped an eyelid and when we went to the desk to leave the room key the dude salesmen demanded to see the manager and proceeded to demand another room, away from the danger of cowboy bullets from below. But the manager told them they had better check out because there were no other rooms available and that he had a long waiting list.

Roy Adams looked down at the two young salesmen, a faint grin on his face. "You're looking at the couple of drunk cowboys who did the shootin'. You dudes want to make somethin' of it, have at it!" The cold chill in Adams' quiet voice scared hell out of the irate traveling salesmen who paid their bill and left in haste, glad to get out of such a madhouse.

In the spring of 1929, Guy hit on a new way of paying tribute to the pioneers who had helped shape the western landscape. Since the first stampede in 1912, Guy had liked nothing better than to bring those cowboys together and listen to their stories about the old days—stories that frequently ended up as articles in his *Billboard* column. He got the idea of having a special dinner to honour these cowmen, and he approached J. J. McGuire, then resident manager of the Canadian Pacific's Palliser Hotel, to see if the Canadian Pacific Railway would be interested in hosting it. As it turned out, the general manager of Canadian Pacific Hotels, H. F. Mathews, was in town, and he promised the company's

full support. The task of assembling those eligible to attend the Rangemen's Dinner, as they decided to call it, would be left up to Guy.

Ranch owners and cowboys, as a breed, were not joiners. They tended to keep pretty much to themselves. But Guy was used to such challenges. Through newspapers, letters and an open column in *Canadian Cattlemen* magazine, Guy announced that the special dinner was "open to anyone who had been actively engaged in the open-range livestock industry, either as an owner, manager, foreman, wagon boss, cowpuncher, horse breaker, cook or horse wrangler, within the area extending from Moose Jaw on the east to Kamloops on the west, and along a line bordering on the Red Deer River on

The Palliser has been the site of the Rangemen's Dinner since 1929. The annual gathering represents the best of ranching experience and knowledge.

the north to the International Boundary line between Canada and the United States on the south, previous to January 2st, 1900, and who at that time was at least 20 years of age." It wasn't long before he was swamped with letters.

Dear Mr. Weadick: Would say I was the first cook on a roundup in Alberta as I first cooked at the Winder ranch in 1878 for Capt. Winder, whose foreman was Charlie Sharples. Next year I cooked for the Walden ranch, John La Mar foreman; next two years with the Oxley ranch, John R. Craig, manager, Jim Patterson, foreman; this was on Willow Creek. Next for Bill Cochrane, then to the Circle with Howell Harris, manager, and Baldy Buck, wagon boss. Also for the McFarlane ranch on the Kootenay River and for George Lane at the Bar U. For further references, ask any oldtimer in Macleod, where I lived from 1874. *Edwin Larkin*

Dear Guy: My qualifications are: I arrived in Alberta in the spring of 1884 and worked for the British American Horse Ranch, a subsidiary of the Cochrane Ranch, the original large one of this country, until July, 1885, after which I have been working for myself, when I took up a ranch west of where Nanton now is, in the latter end of the winter of 1886, and have been engaged in ranching there since....There were a good many outfits taking part in the early roundups on the open range. The one I was particularly identified with, was known as the one conducted by the Mosquito Creek wagon which represented a combination of...outfits. I became wagon boss of this outfit on the roundup in 1889 or '90. Trust this fills the bill. *A. E. Cross*

Dear Weadick: Will you be so kind as to put my name down for the C.P.R. dinner on July 9, 1929. I started cowpunching in 1883 for the JR outfit at Deer Lodge, Montana. Trailed in cattle to Alberta with Tom Lynch in 1884, bringing in the Z and House and 02 cattle. I joined with the Scouts in the Rebellion in 1885 for General T. B. Strange, manager of the House Ranch, and since that time have been running my own outfit, the D I O. *Bob Newbolt*

Attendance secured, Guy turned to the menu. Backed by the talent of J. J. McGuire's staff at the Palliser, he described the food to be served at the first Rangemen's Dinner with the flair of a cow camp cook:

Grub Pile!!!

"Come an' get it or we'll Throw it All Out!!!"

Alberta Celery and Italian Olives

Open Range Beef Boullion and Wedding Rice

Dutch Oven Nester Chicken with Shamrock Bacon and
    Cow Camp Corn Fritters

Canuck Peas with Mint and Campfire Fired Potatoes

Leaf lettuce and Dandelion Salad with Sage Hen Egg Dressing

Frontier Corn Cake with Golden Syrup

Water from the spring in the back.

(If you can beat it, produce!)

Special Notice: After the usual gab during the meal, everybody go up to the
    bed wagon on the cutback where the augerin' and irregatin' plans will be
    gone into in detail.

The dinner, held during stampede week, was a vintage Weadick event, served up with western spirits and storytelling that lasted well into the early morning. The CPR was pleased, and the dinner became an annual event, pausing between 1943 and 1945. The dinner is now run by volunteers on a pay-as-you-go basis, but the cowboys and ranchers still come. In 1994, the Rangemen's Dinner presented a special plaque to Longview rancher Bert Sheppard, who had looked on wide-eyed at the very first stampede.

As the 1920s drew to a close, Guy was riding high, doing the work he loved and promoting everywhere the stampede and the cowboy spirit.

Despite injury, bruises and broken bones, bronc riders continued to take on the odds at the Stampede.

The Last Stampede

THE 1920S WERE GOOD to the Weadicks. Guy was living and breathing the western life he adored. The stampede took up his active time from April to September, while Florence managed the dude ranch. As soon as the stampede closed, the Weadicks spent their time getting the ranch ready for the winter, building new sheds, feeding cattle and caring for stock. But the quiet of the ranch, often snowbound at the end of a rutted gravel road, made Guy restless. He escaped to his small log "office" across the yard from the ranch kitchen, where he would work on saddles, read or peck out endless letters on his old typewriter. After Christmas, he and Florence would take to the road and the vaudeville circuit, often stopping off in Minnesota to visit Florence's father or in Wyoming to visit Guy's brother Tom and his wife, Kitty. It was a gypsy life with one central theme: the Calgary Stampede.

But by the end of the decade, shadows were falling across Guy's path. Vaudeville had begun to fade with the arrival of the "talkies" and other forms of entertainment, and by 1931 it was dead. While there was no welcoming circle of actors and audiences waiting in the wings for Weadick & LaDue on the theatrical run, there were still plenty of old friends to visit. With the resources from the ranch and Guy's stampede salary, Guy and Florence were comfortable gypsies for the next few years.

Their travels across the United States shielded them from the signs of a changing economic situation in Calgary. The 1929 stampede had enjoyed a strong success, reaching new heights in attendance, income and profits. But Ernie Richardson was sobered by the signs of trouble ahead. A new racetrack in Butte, Montana, had drained away much of Calgary's racing profits during the year, and while the stampede attendance was high, expenditures were also rising alarmingly. Downtown merchants were grumbling about the extra work it took to decorate their shops and the way the show impeded entry to their businesses. Following the Wall Street crash of 1929, oil stock plummeted, the price of wheat dropped and jobless single men began crowding Calgary's streets, clamouring for work.

Attendance at the 1930 Calgary Exhibition and Stampede dropped by 56,000; receipts were down $57,000, and the $41,846 profit of 1929 disappeared in a $14,000 deficit. Despite this discouraging performance, the Exhibition and Stampede Board began planning the 1931 stampede with special enthusiasm. It was to be an outstanding tribute to one of their own and one of the biggest birthday parties the country had ever seen: Pat Burns, rancher, businessman, patron of a hundred Calgary causes and legendary member of the Big Four, was turning seventy-five on opening day.

For one week in 1931, Calgary forgot the Depression and celebrated. A growing force of unemployed were given a week's work as ushers, ticket-takers, gate keepers and artisans. Thousands ignored the rain and cheered warmly as Pat Burns took the stage as the grand marshal of the parade. Fifteen thousand people enjoyed pieces of his birthday cake, and seven hundred enjoyed a birthday banquet at which his appointment to the Canadian Senate was announced. Nevertheless, the overall deficit for 1931 was $16,364.

Guy and Florence made the usual rounds of old friends and western celebrities that winter. They dropped in on Walt Coburn and Peter Kyne, Ed Borein, actor William S. Hart and Major Gordon "Pawnee Bill" Lillie at his ranch in Oklahoma. These visits bolstered Guy's confidence even as the Stampede Board cut his salary. He began planning the 1932 stampede, which would be the twentieth anniversary of the event he had created.

Yet the signs of recession were there, and even Guy's inherent optimism couldn't fail to notice them. In 1932, the western world was shocked to learn that the Miller Brothers' fabulous 101 Ranch empire was in liquidation. Western actors like Tom Mix had difficulty making the transition to talking pictures. For a time, Mix left the screen and toured with the Sells-Floto circus, even starting a circus of his own. He made his last film in 1934.

In April 1932, another chapter in Guy's life closed when he learned of the death of his first partner in the Wild West business. Bill Pickett, the Dusky Demon, had been breaking horses at the 101 Ranch when he was kicked by one of the animals. He died hours later.

Guy and Ernie Richardson continued to plan the line-up for the summer 1932 show. Richardson was enthusiastic but cautious. He was pleased to have lined up Duncan's Collies, "the most wonderful animal act in existence," and a five-girl act, the Juggling Jewels, which had been the hit of the Toronto Exhibition. He was able to secure the Princess Patricia's Band for a little over $2,000. Guy continued to promote and talk up the stampede as much as ever, but he was getting tired. The long days on the road were beginning to take their toll. He was saddened, too, by the death of A. E. Cross that spring. There was no talk of celebrating the twenty years of work Guy had put in, no recognition of his role in starting the stampede and making it work all these years. Instead it was cost-cutting, prize reductions and shorter expenses. He saw this cheese-paring as a waste of time, and it was cramping his style.

By March, Guy and Florence were back on the ranch, and Guy was engaged in a running battle with Ernie Richardson over the budget for that year's stampede. Richardson needed to cut expenses, and Guy was adamant any such reduction would result in a "second-class" show. He urged Richardson and the board not to compromise any aspect of the stampede. "The reason we have been able to present a show of that nature, that is considered second to none in the world," he wrote, "is because we have had the finest talent possible. The reason we get them is because we pay the money in purses to draw them…Any attempt to cut purses or do anything that will lower the style of quality of performance we have offered, will result in a falling off of attendance."

His vaudeville work gone and relations with the Exhibition and Stampede Board deteriorating, Guy turned his hopes to the ranch. He applied for copyright on the name "Stampede." He had to hire a lawyer before the Exhibition Board would give its permission to a limited use of the word in relation to Guy's company. One of the conditions the board set was that Guy would not conduct any Wild West shows or similar enterprises in western Canada without the consent in writing of the Calgary Industrial Exhibition Company. Guy and Florence also agreed to give the Exhibition Board the right to secure the name back if they sold the ranch.

Plans went ahead for the 1932 show, but without a unifying event such as Pat Burns's birthday, and with the new strict emphasis on thrift, spirits were low. After almost ten years of spending money to make money, the Calgary Industrial Exhibition began wide-sweeping budget cuts in every area of the operation. Staff salaries had already been reduced by 10 per cent for Richardson and Weadick as well as for clerical employees. Race purses, parade expenses and other attractions had all been reduced in 1931, but these were cut again, along with everything else. The biggest cuts of all were where the largest growth had been—in stampede prizes and expenses.

Guy was convinced the stampede was headed for disaster. He told the Exhibition Board and anyone else who would listen that there was no way cowboys would turn up to compete for the measly prizes being offered. The stampede would flop, and flop big. Many were convinced that Guy had been drinking too much and tried to stave off his fears. But Guy wouldn't be appeased, and he began missing meetings and not showing up at the office.

His heart just wasn't in the thousand and one details that he knew needed

Bronc rider and movie stunt man Yakima Canutt on White Sox at the 1919 Stampede.

attending to. His posted instructions sounded more like old vaudeville theatre edicts than his usual dashing bucked-up vigour: "To Parade Contestants: Make Plenty of Noise, this is Western Week. To All Contestants, watch the daily notices. Do not embarrass your friends by asking them to come into the infield as it will positively not be allowed. It is absolutely imperative that contestants be dressed in cowboy attire both in the parade and in the arena. If you are disqualified for the infraction of any rule, don't claim ignorance." But the show opened on time and to good attendance. While the numbers were down from 1931, there was a good showing of cowboy contestants, particularly

Canadian hands who were eager to compete for whatever prizes were to be had. As James Gray put it in *A Brand of Its Own*, "Weadick, in simple truth, had misread the nature of the cowboy who would challenge a bucking horse for 'pennies, marbles or chalk' if fancier prizes were not available."

Despite the show's success, Guy felt betrayed and unappreciated. He told people he would be all through with the stampede at the end of the week; next year, he might put on another stampede close to Calgary on the same dates as the exhibition, or he might work with the Great Falls folks to put on a big stampede there on the Calgary dates. He was fed up with the Exhibition Board and didn't see why he should take directions from them.

By the evening of July 16, the final night of the stampede, Guy's frustrations had reached the boiling point. He had been drinking earlier in the day, and around 8:30 in the evening he got into a shouting match with E. L. Richardson at the race judges' stand. When it came time for the presentations to be made to the champions, Board Chairman Guy Herbert tried to persuade Guy not to go up onto the platform. But Guy insisted, saying that he was going to go up and "tell the whole rotten bunch of you off…I'm going to tell the crowd that they can take the show and keep it, for I'm through, after tonight."

Guy called the winners out onto the platform according to the arrangements. However, ignoring the special guests who were supposed to make the presentations, Guy swept off his hat and proceeded to introduce each cowboy himself. His unpredictable behaviour during the previous week had prompted Richardson to issue instructions that the microphone was to be turned off if Guy attempted to make any unusual speeches during the final ceremonies. So, in the midst of his speeches to the cowboys, the microphone went dead. It took Guy a moment or two to realize what had happened, and once he did, he continued to talk to the crowd, yelling out, "I put on your first stampede and I've just put on your last."

The incident left everyone with a bad feeling. Newspaper reports on the stampede were terse and economical, with no mention of the final ruckus. By most accounts the show had been a success. But more sobering news was delivered a month later in a front-page statement published in the *Calgary Herald*: "The office of Stampede Manager of the Calgary Exhibition

A Loyal Friend

As word spread about Guy's dismissal as Stampede manager, friends came to his support. From California, the articulate Walt Coburn adopted an aw-shucks voice in a letter to the Exhibition Board: "The rumor has sifted down into the Southwest cow country that you folks are talking about dispensing with the services of Guy Weadick…I sure hope that the news is wrong and that mebbyso it is just some kind of a josh. Because without Guy up there to ramrod the show, it wouldn't seem like home to a lot of boys that sort of associate Guy Weadick with the Calgary Stampede the same way Santy Claus is tied up with Christmas…If you folks fire him, for economic reasons or otherwise, it sure will be a gut-shot to a lot of us."

and Stampede has been dispensed with, and the Stampede, in the future will be managed from the general offices, in line with all other departments of the Exhibition."

Guy had already received word of the board's decision in a registered letter from E. L. Richardson sent August 16. He responded immediately and with heat. He hired the Calgary firm of Andrew Naismith and A. L. Smith to sue the Exhibition Company for $100,000, citing breach of contract and unfair dismissal.

Guy and Florence returned to the ranch to await the result of the law suit, which as it turned out would not be settled for another three years. Guy began quietly feeling out opportunities for organizing other stampedes. On September 17, his Rowdy Waddy "Corral" column in *Billboard* made no mention of the dismissal but announced that: "Guy Weadick has made a marvellous success of The Stampede in connection with Calgary (Alta.) Exhibition. In fact, of late years, Guy, outside of his Stampede Ranch operation in Alberta, has devoted practically all his Wild West sports activities to the annual Calgary event. As he has proven an outstanding success and incidentally, has received numerous attractive offers during the last decade to produce special rodeos—in the United States, Canada and England—wonder if Guy could be induced by some enterprising auspices to stage a big indoor event at some large city over the coming winter? Surely it would be more helpful than harmful to his Stampede connections in Calgary."

Guy was nearly fifty. He was tired, discouraged and bitter. All the arenas he had shone in and worked for all his life were closing. The vaudeville circuit had given up the stage to movies. The movies he had once been familiar with were now being produced in big Hollywood studios. The bright stars of the Wild West shows had retired or gone out of business. And now the stampede, which had been his life, had turned on him. It was hard to see what lay ahead.

Working on the ranch
provided comfort for
Guy and Florence after
the bitter parting with
Stampede officials.

Later Years

WHILE HE WAITED IMPATIENTLY for a court date—the chance to tell his story and clear himself—Guy put a philosophic face on his troubles. In a letter to a friend, he wrote:

We are going to try and keep right on eating, taking a drink when we feel we need one and in general try and conduct ourselves as we have in the past…I've been through some hard times in the past and always got through in the end, although the trail was pretty tough sometimes, and I can look back and see some pretty hard roads I've been over. They may have some tougher ones ahead, but I hardly think so.—and if they should be tougher, I'll try and make the grade anyway.

Guy continued to write, pecking out articles and manuscripts on his type-writer and firing them off to magazines and publishing houses across the country. He was contracted by Doubleday Doran and Co. to produce a series of articles called "Cowboys I Have Known" for their magazine *West*. He worked on stories about Will Rogers and the western writer Will James and about Canadian riders such as Tom Three Persons, Bob Carry, Herman Linder and the Watrin boys.

West magazine also appointed Guy "Range Boss" for a new Range Riders' Club designed to "bring together all people interested in the West." Guy took on the project with his usual energy and quickly signed up an illustrious advisory board, including Frazier Hunt, Peter B. Kyne, William S. Hart and Will James. For Guy it was a lifeline to old friends and the goings-on in cattle country. Letters poured in, describing rodeos, horse sales, news of retired cowhands, even arrivals of the new offspring of famous horses.

In the spring of 1935, Guy received vindication. The Honourable Mr. Justice Ives delivered an oral judgement that "in his opinion the evidence does not warrant a finding that there was any reasonable cause for this dismissal." To the Exhibition Board, Judge Ives was sharp in his pronouncement:

> These men know life pretty well I should say. They must have realized that the position occupied by this Plaintiff was such that it necessitated on his part the indulgence in much more alcohol than was required of other employees. They, I think recognized or believed, whether rightly or wrongly, that his drinking with guests and with contestants and with those connected with the Stampede, promoted generally the welfare of the Stampede…and their evidence of what occurred on Saturday night in no way proved that the Defendant's directors need have been under any misapprehension as to its result on their business and on their future exhibitions and Stampede.

Guy was awarded six months' salary and $1700 in costs. He was exultant, he wrote to a close friend, Banff businessman Norman Luxton. "I am thoroughly satisfied. It was brought out in open court and on the records, exactly why I was fired, Not because I was drinking, but because they objected to me using the title 'The Stampede Ranch Limited' for my ranch company—and as the Judge so aptly put it…they thought that after having me around 10 years…they could do the work and save what they were paying me."

Shortly after the announcement, Guy agreed to stage a rodeo in Lethbridge to celebrate the town's Jubilee celebration, and he threw all his energies into promoting the event, including leading the two-mile parade pageant. He was pleased as punch with the results. The town of 15,000 attracted 42,000 paid admissions over three days and packed the bleachers for every event.

Despite the outcome of the court case, relations with the Exhibition Board still rankled. Guy hadn't set foot on the grounds since 1932, but he was always eager to hear how the stampede was faring. He listened faithfully to the radio announcements of stampede events and kept up to date on changes and additions to the program.

Letters became Guy's link with the western world. He wrote as he spoke, with a fresh conversational style that rarely allowed anyone else to interject. He needed to keep up on rodeo and stampede affairs for his column in *West* magazine. His column recorded forthcoming events, but he never included the Calgary Stampede in his announcements. "Of course the Calgary outfit don't correspond with me," he wrote to Norman Luxton, "and of course it is not up to me to go out of my way to give them publicity. Its a dam cinch they never took any pains to do me any good, so why should I? Am I right or am I right?"

Finances were tight, but Guy didn't seem too concerned. "Income taxes don't bother me, as I have no income," he told a friend. For the next few years, Guy and Florence followed their usual schedule of tending the ranch during the spring and summer and travelling south in winter to visit family and friends.

Guy continued to avoid the stampede, travelling to Calgary during July only to attend the annual Rangemen's Dinner. He was interested in the new rules for rodeo being drawn up by the Turtles Association, a group of cowboys who had organized a strike against American rodeo producer George Johnson in Boston in 1936. Their demands marked the end of the era of old-time independent producers and the establishment of a professional rodeo circuit.

Banff businessman and adventurer Norman Luxton was a close friend of Guy's and shared Guy's interest in promoting the cowboy life and traditions of the First Nations of the West.

Warm Wishes

Guy's contribution to the Calgary Stampede was warmly recognized in a special testimonial prepared by his friends and admirers as a going away gift. It was one of the many tributes Guy and Florence received as they prepared to leave the foothills for Phoenix in 1950. The roster of names included politicians, ranchers, cowboys, businessmen, writers, performers and competitors, illustrating the depth of the friendships Guy had earned in his twenty years with the Stampede.

In 1937, Guy was hired to produce a rodeo at Minot, North Dakota. "The Minot show went over great," he wrote to Norman Luxton afterwards. "I have several different localities in the States whose representatives were at Minot dealing for me to put on some Stampedes in 1938. I turned three down for later this summer, because I just could not spare the time from the ranch."

By the 1940s, Guy had recovered his natural optimism and was putting new energy into the Stampede Ranch. He designed elaborate new letterhead and made plans to promote the ranch all over the United States and eastern Canada.

A lengthy article about Guy was serialized in two issues of *Canadian Cattleman* in 1946. The magazine's editor and author of the article, Ken Coppock, recommended a "Weadick Day" at the stampede as a fitting tribute to its colourful founder. Guy was gratified by the attention, but he felt ambivalent about the recognition. The wound caused by friction with the Exhibition Board was still raw.

In the fall of 1946, Florence was admitted to Calgary's Holy Cross Hospital for an operation. Guy himself was warned to take it easy because of a potential heart condition. After Florence was released, she and Guy reluctantly decided to take doctor's orders and slow down. In the spring of 1947, they sold the Stampede Ranch to Dick Caldwell and his sister Ruby Machin.

After twenty years of calling the foothills their home, Weadick and LaDue were on the road again. They walked away from the ranch clean, leaving rooms full of furniture and memories. On July 13, 1947, they signed the guest book:

Flores LaDue Weadick
Address: The World
Remarks: The finest bunch I ever met

Guy Weadick
Address: Any Place I now Hang my Hat
Remarks: This ranch was my Home for 27 years. To the Caldwells & Machins Good Luck always to "you" from "Me."

Guy and Florence moved first to High River, where they bought a small home with a view sweeping to the foothills. They were welcome in the community and quickly became active in town life. Guy wrote articles for the *High River Times*, reporting on the Western Stock Growers Association meetings, on a new riding and roping club in nearby Black Diamond or on the kick-off of the Southern Alberta Rodeo Circuit. He gave one of the longest talks the Rotary Club had ever heard. He was put in charge of public relations for the High River Rodeo, and later became honorary president. The rodeo was held the weekend before the Calgary Stampede, and it always drew top riders.

The Weadicks continued to winter in Arizona and California, scouting out a place where they could put down roots. The foothills were their home and would remain so all their lives, but their health called for dry, hot weather. In 1950, they finally settled on Phoenix.

They didn't get away from High River quietly. An invitation to a farewell celebration in honour of the Weadicks was issued on the front page of the town's newspaper. A crowd of more than 300 ranchers, farmers, Indians, cowboys, businessmen from Calgary and representatives from districts throughout the province gathered to say good-bye. The couple were presented with an array of gifts. Guy received a solid gold cigarette case engraved with the inscription, "His countless friends and admirers will always remember that it was Guy Weadick who originated and gave to the world, the famous Calgary Stampede." Florence received a gold wrist watch engraved simply, "To a real partner."

Guy launched into a thank-you speech that threatened to outdo his Rotary Club performance until someone yelled, "For god's sake, open the case, Guy!" He did, and for one legendary moment was struck speechless. Inside was a cheque for $10,000. The money, a gift from friends across the country, had been gathered in secret within a few days. It was an astounding representation of the gratitude and respect Guy and Florence had gathered during their life in the Alberta foothills.

In a front-page letter in the *High River Times*, Guy made a parting suggestion. The beautiful natural river park in town, he pointed out, was a gift to the community from the late George Lane of Bar U fame. Why not return the favour and name it "The George Lane Memorial Park"? He and Florence would be pleased to return and help erect a suitable marker.

Guy and Florence moved to Phoenix, but Guy didn't take to retirement. He had written earlier in *Canadian Cattlemen* that "when a cow-puncher quits 'for good' as a rule he is never quite content, unless located in a stock country where he can still meet and talk with people who speak his language." Guy and Florence attended stock sales, rodeo events and western roundups in between visits from family and friends. In January 1951, Guy began a column called "Cowboy News of Range and Arena" for *Canadian Cattlemen*. It allowed him to do what he did best—introduce western stockmen to each other and keep up with the latest news of the western range.

The following June found Florence and Guy back in High River for the naming of the new park. Guy was also interested in developing the historic cattle trail between Fort Benton, Montana, and Macleod, Alberta. The Fort Benton-Macleod Trail, extending as far north as Edmonton, had the same kind of historical importance to that part of the country as the Old Chisholm Trail, he pointed out.

A few days after the naming ceremony, Florence had a severe heart attack, frightening them both. She went into the High River Hospital, where she was told she needed to remain in bed for three to four weeks. Guy was shocked and worried, but his natural optimism took over. By August 6, Florence had recovered enough to enjoy the flowers people had sent, and she encouraged Guy to head south while she recuperated. He made plans to leave, but by the next day, Florence was dead.

Florence was buried in High River, next to her father, Charles Bensell, who had lived with them on the ranch in his later years. Her grave marker was inscribed simply to "A true partner." Guy was devastated by his loss. He returned to Phoenix but was frighteningly alone in the home where he and Florence had planned "to get some rest and real enjoyment in our declining years after a life of toil and hard work." November was a particularly difficult month—it would have been their forty-fifth wedding anniversary.

Guy was encouraged and supported by letters from friends all over North America. "It makes me very happy to know that so many people held Florence in such high regard," he wrote to Jim Cross. "I know it would please her to know she has so many friends, a few of whom she has not seen in years who thought so much of her. Much of any success I have ever had is mostly due to her tolerance, advice and steadying influence she had on me whom she understood so well, far better than I understood myself. I miss her more every day."

The only thing that interested Guy now was tracking down items for Jim Cross's proposed western museum. Cross was the son of A. E. Cross, one of the Big Four, and he was planning to open a Horseman's Hall of Fame in Calgary. Guy wrote, "I was wondering if the silver mounted saddle the Big Four presented me in 1912 would be suitable for your museum. The silver plate bearing the inscription is still on it. I have used the saddle ever since, all over Europe the States and Canada and on the ranch. I have it here, but don't think I'll ever do much riding again."

In 1952 Guy was invited to the Calgary Stampede. It was the first real olive branch in more than twenty years, and he seized on it with relief and pleasure. It would be the fortieth anniversary of the first stampede, and Guy was to be an honoured guest and ride in the parade. Eager to help promote the stampede again, he began gathering material from former world champions such as Ed Echols and Fanny Sperry-Steele for Cross's museum. Dolly Mullens Mott, Florence's old friend and competitor in the first stampede, offered to donate her prize buckle for the World's Championship in Ladies Trick Riding.

Dolly Mott was now a widow living in Los Angeles. She had kept in contact with the Weadicks over the years, and after Florence died Dolly and Guy became closer. On April 4, 1952, she and Guy Weadick were married in Nogales, Mexico, in a civil ceremony. The marriage helped ease Guy's loneliness, but he continued to miss Florence and couldn't help wishing she could attend the anniversary stampede with him. She would always be his true partner.

The 1952 stampede with Guy and Dolly as guests of honour was a record-breaker and a proud moment for Guy. Attendance was over 450,000, the highest ever. Guy led the parade along with Calgary Mayor D. H. Mackay and George Edworthy, president of the Stampede board. Following close behind were cowboys and cowgirls who had taken part in the first show— Clem Gardner, who had won the All-Round Canadian Cowboy title in 1912,

Guy's conversation had one theme: the cowboy life. Whether he was talking about the life of old-time cowboys, passing on news of rodeo performers or reminiscing about western movie stars, Guy kept the memories green.

steer-roping champion Ed Echols, and Bert Weir of Montana, another top roper. Dolly Mullens Weadick represented the cowgirls.

There had been a lot of changes in forty years. The prize money for the saddle bronc event had doubled to $3,500. Women had disappeared from the competition, and trick riding and roping were restricted to exhibitions. The chuckwagon races had become one of the biggest draws. The saddle bronc contest was still the main event, and Guy and other old-timers who remembered Tom Three Persons's epic ride were delighted when Canadian bronc rider Frank Duce from Cardston stole the championship away from the tough American riders, including the legendary Casey Tibbs.

From July 7 to 12, Guy made the rounds, visiting old friends and recalling the early days of the stampede. One of the highlights was a reunion with 160 old-time cowboys at the Rangemen's Dinner at the Palliser. At the dinner, he and Dolly presented Jim Cross with the two gold buckles Dolly and Florence had won at the first stampede.

The 1952 event mended the twenty-year rift between Guy Weadick and the Calgary Stampede. Guy could now take pride in seeing how far his dream had come and how much it was appreciated by new generations of western lovers.

Back in Phoenix, Guy began work on a book about cowboys. He attempted to interest several publishers in it but had no takers. He continued to search out material for Jim Cross. He still hankered after people who could speak his language, and he kept in touch with the Bews family, whose Y Cross Ranch adjoined the Stampede Ranch. Joe Bews had agreed to keep the Weadicks' favourite horses, Snip and Somber. Guy was clear in his directions for the care of the animals: "I do not want the two horses separated. They've run together all their lives and are happy there."

By October 1953, Guy and Dolly had separated. Theirs had been an uneasy marriage. Dolly, irritated by the shadow of Florence, was often acrimonious and had unstable nerves. After more than forty years with Florence, Guy couldn't live with anyone else. He was lonely and frustrated and uncertain of where to turn next. He made arrangements to sell his house in Phoenix and talked about doing radio and television work in Hollywood. In December, he received the good news that Snip had had a colt, which the

Bews family had named "Miss Weadick." Guy was delighted, and he promised to come up and see her.

On December 15, 1953, Lou Bradley, one of Guy and Florence's High River friends, received a phone call from Guy's brother Tom in Los Angeles. Guy was dead. Lou was shocked; he had received a letter from Guy just the day before, in which Guy had talked about going on television at the beginning of the new year. He had sounded confident and was looking forward to the future. It was unclear at first how Guy had died, and some felt that his rocky relationship with Dolly had contributed to his death.

The funeral services were held in High River, according to Guy's wishes. It was an enormous funeral; more than five hundred people turned out to pay their respects, including the members of the Calgary Exhibition and Stampede Board. Bleak, wintry skies clouded the procession, which was led by Joe Bews and Guy's horse Snip. Guy's boots were placed backwards in the stirrups of the riderless horse, symbolizing long remembrance of the owner among his ranching friends. The saddle on the mare had been a gift from the Big Four, and the bridle a gift from the Prince of Wales. Following Snip was the new foal, Miss Weadick.

Active pallbearers were drawn from the ranchers Guy knew as neighbours and friends, and the memorial service was held in the hall where Guy and Florence had been given a send-off three years earlier. After the service, Guy Weadick was laid to rest beside his beloved Florence in the High River cemetery. His grave marker reads, "Guy George Weadick, founder of the Calgary Stampede and loyal son of his adopted west."

Guy Weadick, loyal son of his adopted West.

The spirit of Guy George Weadick continues to blow through the western foothills.

In 1958, an "I Rode With Guy Weadick" rodeo in High River saw cowboys from Arizona, Texas, New Mexico, Wyoming, Colorado, Washington, Idaho, Saskatchewan, British Columbia and all over Alberta gather for a reunion and tribute to the great rodeo promoter. More than forty former contestants led the parade on horseback, and following the parade, the members of the reunion went to the cemetery to pay their respects. Clem Gardner placed a wreath on Guy's grave.

Fifty years after the first stampede, the Calgary Exhibition and Stampede invited friends, relatives and associates to attend the unveiling of a bronze memorial tablet to Guy's memory in the Big Four building on the Stampede Grounds.

In 1979, it was announced that "the memory of the late Guy Weadick, originator and first manager of the Calgary Stampede, will be perpetuated through an annual trophy award starting at this year's Stampede." The Guy Weadick Memorial Trophy is awarded to the rodeo contestant who best exemplifies the cowboy of today. The trophy, along with a $100 cash prize, is given to the cowboy who combines ability, sportsmanship, dress and showmanship.

In 1982, seventy years after he had staged the first stampede, Guy Weadick was inducted into the Canadian Rodeo Historical Association's Hall of Fame.

Epilogue

Sources

Selected Books

Abbott, E. D. ("Teddy Blue") and Smith, Helena Huntington. *We Pointed Them North*. (Norman: University of Oklahoma Press) 1955

Adams, Andy. *The Log of a Cowboy*. (Boston: Houghton Mifflin) 1903

Athearn, Robert T. *The Mythic West in Twentieth-Century America*. (Kansas: University of Kansas Press) 1986

Bower, B. M. *Chip of the Flying U*. (New York: G. W. Dillingham) 1904

Borein, E. *Etchings of the West*. Edited by Edward S. Spaulding. (Santa Barbara: Edward Borein Memorial) 1950

Byers, Chester. *Cowboy Roping and Rope Tricks*. (New York: Dover Publications) 1966

Clancy, Foghorn. *My Fifty Years in Rodeo*. (San Antonio: The Naylor Company) 1952

Coburn, Wallace David. *Rhymes from a Round-Up Camp*. (New York, London: G. P. Putnam's Sons) 1903

Collings, Ellsworth. *The 101 Ranch*. (Norman: University of Oklahoma) 1937

Demeglio, John E. *Vaudeville U.S.A.* (Bowling Green: University Popular Press) 1973

Dempsey, Hugh A. *History in Their Blood*. (Vancouver: Douglas & McIntyre) 1982

Evans, Simon. *Prince Charming Goes West*. (Calgary: University of Calgary Press) 1993

Faulknor, Cliff. *Turn Him Loose! Herman Linder, Canada's Mr. Rodeo.* (Saskatoon: Western Producer Prairie Books) 1977

Foran, Max, and Jameson, Sheilagh, eds. *Citymakers.* (Calgary: Alberta Historical Society, Chinook Country Chapter) 1987

Fredriksson, Kristine. *American Rodeo from Buffalo Bill to Big Business.* (Texas: A&M University Press) 1985

Goetzmann, William H. and Goetzmann, William N. *The West of the Imagination.* (New York, London: W. W. Norton & Company) 1986

Gray, James H. *A Brand of Its Own: The 100 Year History of the Calgary Exhibition and Stampede.* (Saskatoon: Western Producer Prairie Books) 1985

Hanes, Col. Bailey C. *Bill Pickett, Bulldogger.* (Norman: University of Oklahoma Press) 1977

Kennedy, Fred. *Alberta Was My Beat: Memoirs of a Western Newspaperman.* (Calgary: The Albertan) 1975

Ketchum, Richard M. *Will Rogers, the Man and His Times.* (New York: American Heritage Publishing Company Inc.) 1973

Knupp, Lillian. *Life and Legends: A History of the Town of High River.* (Calgary: Sandstone Publishing) 1982

Lecompte, Mary Lou. *Cowgirls of the Rodeo.* (Urbana and Chicago: University of Illinois Press) 1993

Mix, Paul E. *The Life and Legend of Tom Mix.* (South Brunswick and New York: A. S. Barnes & Company) 1972

Nelson, Doug. *From Hotcakes to High Stakes: The Chuckwagon Story.* (Calgary: Detselig) 1993

North, Escott. *The Saga of the Cowboy.* Introduction by Guy Weadick. (London: Jarrolds Publishers) 1942

Palmer, Howard, with Tamara Palmer. *Alberta: A New History.* (Edmonton: Hurtig Publishers) 1990

Patterson, R. M. *Far Pastures.* (Vancouver: Evergreen Press) 1963

Roosevelt, Theodore. *Ranch Life and the Hunting-Trail.* (New York: The Century Co.) 1888

Russell, Charles M. *Good Medicine.* (New York: Doubleday, Doran & Co.) 1930

Russell, Don. *The Wild West.* (Norman: University of Oklahoma) 1970

Sheppard, Bert. *Spitzee Days.* (Altona: D.W. Friesen) 1988

———*Just about Nothing.* (Calgary. McAra Printing) 1977

Stein, Charles. ed. *American Vaudeville as Seen by Its Contemporaries.* (New York: Alfred A. Knopf) 1984

Taylor, Lonn and Marr, Ingrid. *The American Cowboy.* (Washington: Library of Congress) 1983

Westermeir, Clifford W. *Man, Beast, Dust: The Story of Rodeo.* (Lincoln: University of Nebraska Press) 1987

Selected Newspapers

Albertan: March 2, 1912; March 30, 1912; December 28, 1931; June 20, 1932; June 7, 1952; December 21, 1953; June 14, 1969.

Calgary Herald: May 17, 1893; July 4, 1905; June 30, 1908; July-September 1912; January 26, 1922; July 29, 1922; July 10, 1923; July 18, 1932; July 9, 1949; July 13, 1982; June 6, 1986.

Calgary News-Telegram: September 2-7, 1912.

Edmonton Bulletin: February 24, 1931.

Havre Plaindealer: October 11, 1919.

High River Times: July 8, 1948; August 17, 1950; August 24, 1950; August 1951; December 24, 1953.

Lethbridge Herald: September 24, 1920; July 4, 1934; July 11, 1935; July 19, 1935; July 26, 1935; July 22, 1936.

New York Times: August 6-15, 1916.

Rochester Democrat and Chronicle: December 19, 1953.

Rochester Times-Union: April 24, 1990.

Winnipeg Tribune: July 31, 1913; August 3-13, 1913.

Periodicals

Canadian Cattlemen: June 1945; June and September 1946; December 1948; March 1949; June 1949.

Frontier Times: February-March 1969.

Rochester History: July 1941.

Vaudeville News: February 26, 1926.

Wild Bunch: August 1975.

Acknowledgements

Guy Weadick cast a long shadow, and I am particularly grateful for the many conversations I was able to have with people who knew him. His niece, Barbara Merback, and her husband, Don, in Caspar, Wyoming, were very helpful with family details and photographs. Cate Cabot Wilson, Guy's great-niece, who looks and talks the way I imagined Guy would look and talk, has been very supportive as well. I am continually grateful to Bert Sheppard, Warren Zimmerman and Betty Zimmerman for their patient and thoughtful answers to my persistent questions. Mary Dover was both delightful and insightful to interview, and Lenore Bews McLean's warmth and encouragement have helped shape the manuscript considerably. Josephine Bews, Marmie Hess and Lillian Knupp were also generous with their recollections.

I am particularly grateful to James Gray's excellent history of the Stampede, *A Brand of Its Own*, and to *Canadian Cattlemen*'s two-part article on Guy Weadick in 1946, as well as to the Guy Weadick, Norman Luxton and Calgary Exhibition and Stampede files in the Glenbow Archives.

I am grateful to the Museum of the Highwood in High River through Lynn Cartwright and to Brad Mason for the loan of his grandfather Lou Bradley's collection of photographs. Fellow researchers Doug Nelson, David Finch, Candace Savage and Dorothy Chansky passed along ideas and encouragement as well. Hugh Dempsey, who is able to answer questions I don't even know how to ask, is an ongoing support.

The Glenbow Museum is a remarkable storehouse of information on the Canadian West. Much of that information is found in the stacks of Library and Archives, but even more is found in the support and encouragement of the professional staff there. My sincere thanks go out to all the staff in the Library and Archives and in the Photography Department for their patience and assistance. It was wonderful to work with a gifted and intelligent editor, Barbara Pulling, whose approach to language is both refreshing and instructive. Lou Palmer has taught me how important it is to give 100 per cent in trick roping and in life.

Joy Harvie Maclaren provides very special support to assist people in realizing their dreams. I am very grateful for her assistance, through the Joy Harvie Maclaren scholarship fund at Glenbow, in researching and writing this book.

As a fisherman's daughter from the West Coast, I find that the ranching community in southern Alberta feels strangely like home. There's an honesty, a quirky individualism, a sense of community and an energy there that I have relied on a lot in writing this book. So for all the cups of coffee in all the ranch-houses, thank you.

And finally, I am constantly grateful to Edward Cavell, a true partner, whose care and good humour makes all things possible.

Photo credits

Facing contents page: Glenbow Archives
NA 446-98

Page x: Museum of the Highwood,
Bradley Collection

Page 5: Glenbow photo: Anita Dammer

Page 7: Museum of the Highwood,
Bradley Collection

Page 8: Buffalo Bill Historical Center

Page 11: Glenbow Archives NB 28-16.
Original photograph in the collection of
the Charles M. Russell Museum,
Montana.

Page 12: Glenbow Archives NA 777-15

Page 14: Glenbow Archives NA 3818-21

Page 16: Glenbow Archives NA 859-1

Page 18: Western History Collections,
University of Oklahoma

Page 20: Western History Collections,
University of Oklahoma

Page 22: Merback Collection

Page 23: Museum of the Highwood,
Bradley Collection

Page 25: Glenbow Archives NA 628-4

Page 26: Merback Collection

Page 31: Glenbow Archives NA 1473-1

Page 33: Museum of the Highwood,
Bradley Collection

Page 34: Glenbow Archives NA 446-99

Page 36: Glenbow Archives NA 2345-19

Page 39: Glenbow Archives NA 3165-26

Page 40: Glenbow Archives NA 1216-1

Page 41: Glenbow Archives NA 4387-8

Page 44: Museum of the Highwood,
Bradley Collection

Page 47: Glenbow Archives NA 446-25

Page 49: Glenbow Archives NB (H) 16-332

Page 50: Glenbow Archives NA 335-60

Page 51: Glenbow Archives NA 778-7

Page 53: Glenbow Archives NA 335-50

Page 54: Glenbow Archives NB 335-18

Page 56: Glenbow Archives NA 1029-18

Page 59: Glenbow Archives NA 1029-12

Page 60: Glenbow Archives NA 1483-9

Page 61: Glenbow Archives NA 3985-6

Page 63: Museum of the Highwood,
Bradley Collection

Page 66: Merback Collection

Page 69: Merback Collection

Page 72: Glenbow Archives NA 1473-22

Page 73: Glenbow Archives NA 3181-47

Page 76: Glenbow Archives NA 1483-7

Page 80: Glenbow Archives NA 1483-8

Page 83: Glenbow Archives NB 2800-13

Page 86: Museum of the Highwood,
Bradley Collection

Page 88: Merback Collection

Page 91: Glenbow Archives NA 3181-71

Page 92: Glenbow Archives NA 446-93

Page 95: Glenbow Archives NA 778-3

Page 99: Glenbow Archives NA 446-132

Page 101: Museum of the Highwood,
Bradley Collection

Page 104: Glenbow Archives NA 462-6

Page 109: Glenbow Archives NA 446-14

Page 112: Museum of the Highwood,
Bradley Collection

Page 115: Glenbow Archives NA 1241-806

Page 116: Glenbow Archives NA 3173-26

Page 120: Museum of the Highwood,
Bradley Collection

Page 123: Glenbow Archives NA 2380-12

Page 124: Glenbow Archives NA 628-1

Page 133: Dean/Cavell

Page 134: Glenbow Archives NA 462-15

About the author

ONNA LIVINGSTONE, a fisherman's daughter from an island off British Columbia's West Coast, found a second home in the ranching community of southern Alberta after discovering that fishers and cowboys have the same quirky independence, bittersweet sense of humour and extraordinary storytelling abilities. She is currently vice-president, program and exhibit development, at the Glenbow Museum in Calgary.